All Scripture references taken from the KJV of the Holy Bible, unless otherwise indicated.

Unguarded Hours: *Standing Watch When the Body Must Rest*

by Dr. Marlene Miles

Freshwater Press 2026
freshwaterpress9@gmail.com

ISBN: 978-1-971933-42-9

Paperback Version

Table of Contents

UNGUARDED HOURS

AUTHOR'S NOTE

This book assumes a degree of spiritual literacy.

It was not written as an introduction to prayer, spiritual life, or discernment, though readers at different stages may encounter it. Some concepts may feel unfamiliar at first—not because they are obscure, but because they are often practiced quietly rather than explained publicly.

This book does not offer formulas, rituals, or guarantees.

It does not ignore spiritual opposition, after all, why would any of us need prayer unless something negatively spiritual, unseen, unknown, or invisible could be happening around us? What is shared here arose from necessity, not preference, and from exhaustion, not ambition.

Readers are encouraged to exercise discernment, restraint, and Wisdom in how they receive what follows.

If you are not in a season of strain, you may read with curiosity rather than adoption.

If you are in a season of strain or oppression, you will recognize what belongs to you.

This book respects both.

PREFACE

There are seasons when strength looks like vigilance. There are seasons when strength looks like rest.

This book was written out of a season when vigilance had been prolonged beyond what was sustainable—not because of disobedience, but because of responsibility. Prayer had been prayed. Fasts had been fasted. Watchfulness had been kept. And still, exhaustion arrived before resolution, before freedom.

What followed was not collapse, but clarity.

It became evident that many people encounter their most vulnerable moments not when they are reckless, but when they are tired. Not when they have abandoned discipline, but when discipline has demanded more than the body can supply.

Scripture does not shame such moments. It addresses them.

Unguarded Hours is not a call to fear the night, avoid rest, or live in heightened suspicion. It is an invitation to order what must remain attentive when consciousness gives way to sleep.

This is a quiet book. It does not shout. It does not rush. It was written for those who know that faithfulness sometimes means staying—and sometimes means sleeping.

And who want to do both wisely.

INTRODUCTION

Somewhere, someone must be awake. While cities sleep and households rest, there has always been someone assigned to stand watch. A watchman on a wall. A guard at a gate. A sentinel on a tower looking into the dark for movement that others cannot see. Nowadays, electronic and digital devices. Of course, those devices only detect what is physical.

There is much more to life than what is seen in the natural.

The watchman does not stand there because danger is certain. He stands there because danger is possible.

Most people do not think about watchfulness in their own lives. They assume that if something serious were approaching, they would notice. But many of life's most consequential moments do not arrive with noise or warning. They arrive quietly — in the unguarded hours.

Many people assume that life becomes dangerous only during obvious crises. To live peacefully I suppose we all have to assume that we live in safety, after all it is a promise from God for those who are His.

That is not always the case, however. Scripture shows the opposite. People often fall when they are tired, even though they feel safe, or when they assume nothing important is happening.

Dangerous moments may not be obvious at all; they may feel Harmless, unless your eyes and neck are on swivel and your discernment is on high alert.

One's guard can be lowered slowing. Imperceptibly by fatigue, distraction, compromise, isolation, and rebellion earlier. Fatigue — when strength is depleted Distraction — when attention shifts away False security — when nothing seems wrong

Deception — when something appears good but isn't

Compromise — small permissions that grow

Neglect — when vigilance fades

Isolation — when correction disappears

Rebellion — stepping outside protection

WHY WE NEED TO BE GUARDED

Many are the afflictions of the righteous but the Lord delivers us out of them all.

Why does man require guarding at all? It's not paranoia, or suspicion, but it's for the protection of something valuable and vulnerable. Man must be guarded. Man requires guarding because he is valuable, permeable, and unfinished. There are enemies out here. Guarding exists because exposure exists.

Unlike God, man is not self-contained. He lives in an environment that can influence him, strengthen him, or weaken him.

Man Is Valuable. We are masterpieces. We are designer originals. Anything valuable requires protection. Whether or not danger is constant, value still attracts attention, influence, interference, and claim.

A person carries life. He carries agency. Influence. Covenant with Almighty God. He carries purpose and destiny. Those things are not trivial. They are priceless; they are worth guarding.

Man is permeable. Human beings are not sealed systems. Thoughts enter. Emotions enter. Ideas enter. Influence enters. Man can be affected by words, environments, relationships. Man is subject to fatigue, fear, deception. Because influence can enter, discernment and guarding are necessary.

Man is still being formed. A finished structure does not require the same protection as one still under construction. Human beings are always learning, adjusting, strengthening, and maturing. Formation means there are seasons of vulnerability. Guarding protects what is as well as what is still developing.

Man lives in time. Humans move through changing seasons, shifting pressures, and varying levels of strength. There are hours when a person is alert, rested, and discerning. There are other hours when a person is tired, distracted, and emotionally exposed. Those are the unguarded hours.

Guarding exists to protect man when his strength fluctuates.

Man Has an Interior Life. The most important parts of a person are not visible. The heart, mind, and spirit are interior spaces.

Scripture repeatedly instructs guarding:

- *Guard your heart* (Proverbs 4:23)
- *Be watchful* (1 Peter 5:8)
- *Take every thought captive* (2 Corinthians 10:5)

Guarding is not merely physical protection; it is governance of the inner life.

A person can be self-Guarded, watchful, disciplined, aware of influence, governing thoughts and choices. Or, a person can be guarded by others, such as family, community, prayer, spiritual covering, and divine protection. Both forms of guarding matter. One does not replace the other.

Man must be guarded because he is valuable, permeable, and still being formed. Influence can enter him, strength can fluctuate within him, and purpose rests upon him. Guarding exists not because man is weak, but because of who he is, whose he is, and what he carries is worth protecting.

Man can fall into a lull and believe he doesn't need to be guarded and so unless someone else is guarding him, these will constitute unguarded hours. There is an enemy of our souls and he is looking for exactly that--, unguarded hours.

The danger appears when attention slips. It happens when fatigue rises, or when discipline relaxes, or watchfulness fades That is when guarding fails.

The enemy wants us unguarded, distracted, weak—easier to attack. *Why*? (Guarding with you, not instead of you…)

MAN IS USEFUL AND NEEDED

Man is not only useful, he is needed.

By whom? By what? ...

By the spirit world. By if not many, all.

Man is not merely a creature placed on the Earth to exist; he is needed.

Needed by whom?

God, who created the Heavens and the Earth, does not need man in the sense of dependence. Scripture makes clear that God lacks nothing. Yet God repeatedly chooses to work through human beings. From the beginning, mankind was given responsibility. Genesis 1:28 shows that humanity was instructed to replenish the Earth and exercise stewardship over it.

Adam was placed in the Garden not only to enjoy it but to tend it and keep it (Genesis 2:15). In other words, the Earth was designed to include human participation.

Man is needed in the order of Creation. Man occupies a particular place within the structure of creation. He is given responsibility, the ability to discern, and the ability to choose. With the authority that man is given, he can wield influence and power or he can give away that authority--, lose it, or neglect it.

It can be taken then.

Without human participation, much of what happens on the Earth simply does not or cannot occur. Scripture often shows God working through people to accomplish His purposes.

Man is needed as a Watchman. Throughout Scripture, people are assigned positions of watchfulness. Watchmen warn of danger. Leaders guide others. Parents guard their children. Believers are instructed to remain alert.

The language of watchfulness appears again and again. He is to watch, guard, keep, and stand. These are not passive roles. They require human attention.

The enemy targets man. If human beings occupy a position of stewardship and authority within creation, then it is understandable why the enemy's efforts often focus on influencing people.

Corrupt the watchman, and the city becomes vulnerable. Distract the steward, and the garden deteriorates. Convince the gatekeeper to sleep, and entry becomes simple.

Man is not needed because God lacks power, Man is needed because God chose to entrust responsibility. The Earth was created for the Glory of God and man is supposed to be one of if not the crowing glory of God. After all, man is created in God's own image and likeness.

Scripture repeatedly describes humans as gatekeepers or watchmen rather than merely observers.

The spirit world cannot legally act in the Earth except by agreement with at least one human. Man is useful, and he is needed. Yet it is well understood that we are not independent of God and neither is God dependent upon us. God is Sovereign.

Scripture consistently shows that **human beings are the ones given stewardship on the Earth**, and many spiritual actions in the Biblical narrative involve some form of **human participation or agreement**. You can see the pattern in passages such as:

- Genesis 1:26-28 — humanity given dominion and stewardship over the earth
- Matthew 18:18 — binding and loosing connected to human authority and agreement
- James 5:16-18 — Elijah praying and events unfolding on Earth
- Luke 10:19 — authority given to Believers over the power of the enemy.

Saints of God, if we have power over the enemy, the works of the enemy then like the Bible says, our Yes is

Yes and our No is No. We can say to the enemy you can or you cannot do whatever you are trying to do.

God is Sovereign. The enemy of our souls is not sovereign. God often chooses to work through human participation rather than bypassing it.

God is sovereign. The devil is not. Scripture makes this clear in many places. For example: Job 1:12. Colossians 1:16-17, 1 John 4:4. Creation exists under God's authority. The enemy does not possess independent rule over Creation.

God governs Creation. Nothing exists outside His knowledge or authority. The heavens belong to Him, and all things ultimately answer to His Will.

His sovereignty means that history is not random and the universe is not controlled by competing equal powers. There is no cosmic rivalry between two equally matched rulers. There is not rivalry between the thing made and the One who made it. There is no comparison of power, authority, or influence. God alone is Sovereign.

The devil is not sovereign. The enemy operates differently. He does not rule Creation, but he manipulates it when he can. The devil influences, tempts, deceives, and opposes—but always within limits.

Scripture repeatedly shows that the enemy cannot act with unrestricted authority. Even in the Book of Job, his activity is clearly bounded.

If the enemy were sovereign, vigilance would be meaningless and we'd be wiped out since his desire is to steal, kill, and destroy. But the devil is not sovereign.

Although the enemy is not sovereign, Scripture still calls believers to watchfulness and resistance. Believers are instructed to be alert, to stand firm, and to guard their lives.

Watchfulness is not based on fear. It is based on responsibility.

God governs Creation, but He also entrusts people with stewardship and calls them to remain attentive.

God is Sovereign. The enemy is opportunistic. God rules the universe. The enemy looks for unattended doors. Therefore, the watchman must man his post.

There are instances where spiritual beings act without human invitation but somewhere, some how an evil entity has been granted permission. It's either invitation in the now or permission through a past, familial, generational or ancestral evil covenant. The dark kingdom is not likely found doing something they should not be doing. If they are, they can be taken to the Courts of the Heaven for that. This is why they present petition of accusation or other evil petitions before the Throne of God to get permission to do evil things in the Earth, as seen in 42 chapters in the Book of Job.

God established the Earth as a realm of human stewardship. Because of that, many spiritual outcomes unfold through human agreement, obedience, or participation.

Man is useful, and man is needed. To be legal in the Earth realm a physical body is needed. A living breathing man has that and is that. From the beginning, the Earth was entrusted to humanity. Dominion was given to people, and responsibility followed that authority.

When people agree with Truth, Truth advances. When people agree with deception, deception gains ground. When people stand watch, gates remain guarded. When people abandon their posts, access becomes opportunity for the devil and his dark kingdom. The enemy understands this well.

He does not need to overthrow creation directly. He only needs to persuade the watchman, distract the watchman. Trick the watchman. Own the watchman.

This is why vigilance matters. And this is why a human life — attentive, discerning, and watchful — is far more significant than many people realize.

Man is useful. Man is needed. By whom? By so many. By so, so many.

The heaven, even the heavens, are the LORD's: but the earth hath he given to the children of men. (Psalm 115:16)

Man is not optional in the functioning of the Earth. God did not merely place humans here as observers; He entrusted them with a sphere of responsibility. The Earth was given to man. The highest Heavens belong to the LORD, but the Earth has been given to mankind. That does not mean the Earth belongs to humanity in an ultimate sense. Everything remains God's Creation. But within the structure of Creation, the Earth was entrusted to human stewardship.

From the beginning, mankind was instructed to replenish the Earth. Cultivate it. Govern it, and guard it.

This responsibility appears as early as Genesis, where Adam is placed in the Garden to tend it and keep it (Genesis 2:15). To keep something means to guard it. The Earth was not designed to function without human watchmen.

If the Earth is entrusted to human stewardship, then human *agreement* matters. The Bible speaks often of agreement. Where the people are one, there God commands the blessing. When two agree as touching. In the mouth of two or three witnesses, let every word be established.

What people welcome, tolerate, encourage, or resist shapes what happens in their lives and in the world around them.

The enemy even understands this structure very well. He does not need to control the Earth directly. He only needs to influence, direct, tempt, or *own* the watchmen.

The Earth was entrusted to mankind. Which means the watchman matters. When the watchman sleeps, the gate becomes easier to enter.

Vigilance is part of the responsibility entrusted to human beings.

> Surely the Lord GOD will do nothing, but he revealeth his secret unto his servants the prophets. (Amos 3:7)

God does not operate in secrecy away from the people He appoints to watch. He involves human beings in what He is doing. God Reveals Before He Acts. Scripture shows that God often reveals His intentions before major events unfold. He speaks, warns, instructs, or prepares those who are listening.

The prophet Amos states plainly that the Lord reveals His secret to His servants before acting.

This pattern appears repeatedly throughout Scripture. Before judgment came upon the Earth, Noah was warned. Before Sodom fell, Abraham was told. Before Egypt was struck with plagues, Moses was *sent.* God did not act silently. He spoke to those who were paying attention. And God's prophets spoke to those who would listen.

If God reveals His intentions to those who are listening, then watchfulness becomes very important. It means that someone must be listening. Someone must be watching. Someone must recognize what is being said. A watchman is not merely a guard; he is someone who pays attention to what others might miss.

When God reveals something, it is not simply information. It carries responsibility. The watchman must understand what he hears. He must remain alert. He must respond appropriately. Revelation without watchfulness accomplishes very little.

God entrusts the Earth to humanity, warns those who are listening, and calls watchmen to remain alert so that the gates of life are not left unguarded.

WHEN SIN WAITS AT THE DOOR

If thou doest well, shalt thou not be accepted? and if thou doest not well, sin lieth at the door. And unto thee shall be his desire, and thou shalt rule over him.
(Genesis 4:7)

A predator is crouching outside the doorway. This is the first doorway moment; it is threshold language. God tells Cain something extremely important: Sin is not inside yet. It is at the door. The door still exists. The threshold is still intact. Cain still has authority. This is a watchman moment.

The enemy is not breaking in; it is waiting. Many spiritual failures do not start with catastrophe. They can start with something as simple as the enemy waiting at the door during an unguarded hour.

"Unto Thee Shall Be His Desire." In other words, sin wants entrance. It wants influence. It wants territory. But the verse does not say sin will win.

"Thou Shalt Rule Over Him." This is the key line. God tells Cain, You still have governing authority.

We all must govern ourselves accordingly. The danger is not the presence of sin. The danger is leaving the door unattended.

People may assume danger arrives after the guard is gone. Genesis shows something deeper: The guard must remain to disallow the danger from entering. If it is allowed entrance, once it crosses the threshold, things change quickly.

Cain ignored the watchman moment — and the story turns tragic immediately afterward. Before Cain ever lifted a hand against his brother, God spoke to him about something far more important: the moment before the act. Sin had not entered his life fully. It was waiting. It crouched at the door like a patient, vigilant predator.

Cain was told two things: 1. It desires you. 2. But you must rule over it. Every life has such moments. Moments when the door is still closed, but something waits outside it. The outcome of those moments often determines the course of everything that follows.

Doing well—approaching God rightly—keeps the door guarded. Scripture suggests several ordinary practices that quietly strengthen a person's "spiritual perimeter," sometimes without us even thinking about it. They are listed next.

1. Worship and Right Offering. Cain and Abel's story already shows this. Worship aligns the heart toward God. Giving something that honors God keeps the heart from hardening. Right worship tends to keep resentment, pride, and bitterness from gaining ground.

2. Obedience in Small Things. Small acts of obedience create a habit of alignment. (Luke 16:10) — faithfulness in little things. James 4:7 — resist the devil. People often think of spiritual warfare as dramatic, but simple obedience already pushes back darkness.

3. Humility. Humility closes doors that pride opens. Pride invites deception. Humility keeps a person teachable.

A humble posture naturally keeps many traps from forming. (James 4:6)

4. Gratitude. Gratitude changes the internal atmosphere. When someone practices thankfulness: Bitterness struggles to grow. Entitlement loses power. Even Paul links thanksgiving with guarding the heart in Philippians 4:6-7.

5. Guarding the Mind. What people dwell on matters. Paul says in Philippians 4:8 to think on what is true, honorable, and pure. When the mind is disciplined, many destructive impulses never gain momentum.

6. Fellowship With the Right People. Isolation weakens discernment. Scripture emphasizes the protection of community:

- Ecclesiastes 4:12
- Hebrews 10:24-25

Being around people who speak truth helps maintain watchfulness.

7. Regular Self-Examination. Checking one's own heart keeps problems from growing unnoticed. Paul encourages this in 2 Corinthians 13:5. Quiet reflection often reveals things before they become serious problems.

8. Restraint. Sometimes protection comes simply from not acting on every impulse. Proverbs praises restraint repeatedly, such as in Proverbs 25:28: Self-control is like a wall around a city.

9. Rest. Even rest can be protective. Fatigue often weakens judgment and patience. Allowing proper rest protects both the body and the inner life.

10. Simple Faithfulness. Showing up consistently—praying, reading Scripture, doing what is right—creates a steady spiritual environment. Faithfulness doesn't feel dramatic, but over time it forms strong defenses.

Many people imagine that protection comes from extraordinary spiritual actions. In reality, much of life's protection grows out of ordinary faithfulness—worship, humility, obedience, gratitude, and quiet attention to the condition of the heart. These simple practices often keep doors closed long before danger arrives.

WHO DROPPED THE GUARD?

The guard rarely drops because someone decides to abandon it. More often it drops through slow, ordinary mechanisms that feel harmless in the moment.

Things that cause the Guard to Drop

Fatigue. When a person is tired, the mind stops watching carefully. Fatigue weakens attention, patience, discernment, and resistance. Even disciplined people make poor decisions when exhausted. As many may know driving tired is considered as or more dangerous than driving inebriated.

Sometimes the guard drops simply because the person needed rest and didn't take it. Fell asleep on the job.

Distraction pulls attention away from what matters. This may be chosen entertainment, unexpected crisis, constant activity, or emotional entanglement. A distracted mind cannot guard well because it is looking elsewhere.

False Security. "Nothing will happen to me." When things have been calm for a long time, people assume the calm is permanent. Confidence becomes carelessness.

Deception. Sometimes the guard drops because something appears harmless. Deception often looks like opportunity, comfort, flattery, or relief. What lowers the guard is not obvious danger — it is misplaced trust. The Gibeonites disguised themselves as completely different people from a distant land and fooled the Israelites.

Gradual Compromise. The guard rarely falls all at once. More often it lowers through small concessions, relaxing a standard, ignoring a warning, or delaying a correction. One small allowance becomes another. Eventually vigilance is gone.

Emotional Turbulence. Strong emotions narrow perception. Fear, anger, grief, excitement, or infatuation can all overwhelm discernment. When emotion governs the moment, the guard weakens.

Isolation. A person who has no trusted voices around them may lose perspective. Guarding becomes harder when no one can question you. no one can warn you. no one sees what you cannot see. Isolation removes external awareness.

Laziness or Neglect. Sometimes the guard drops simply because maintaining awareness requires effort. Watchfulness is a form of discipline. Neglect — even small neglect — opens gaps.

The guard rarely drops in dramatic moments. It lowers quietly through fatigue, distraction, misplaced trust, and small compromises. What is neglected for a moment can become exposed for a season.

The guard does not fail only in extreme situations. Most vulnerability comes from ordinary human conditions

Once the guard drops, is it gone forever?

No. Well, hopefully not. Return to your post. Vigilance must return.

Scripture is not silent about the moments when vigilance failed. Many of the people we admire in the Bible experienced seasons when their guard dropped — sometimes through fatigue, sometimes through distraction, sometimes through misplaced trust. These accounts are not recorded to shame them. They are recorded so we can recognize the same patterns in ourselves and guard our lives more wisely.

Scripture is not silent about the moments when vigilance failed. Many of the people we admire in the Bible experienced seasons when their guard dropped — sometimes through fatigue, sometimes through distraction, sometimes through misplaced trust. These accounts are not recorded to shame them. They are recorded so we can recognize the same patterns in ourselves and guard our lives more wisely.

BIBLICAL EXAMPLES OF THE GUARD DROPPING

Fatigue — Elijah After Mount Carmel. In 1 Kings 19 after the great victory over the prophets of Baal, Elijah collapses emotionally when Jezebel threatens him.

He says, "It is enough; now, O LORD, take away my life." Elijah had just experienced one of the greatest victories in Scripture, yet exhaustion weakened his resilience.

God's first response was not correction — it was rest, food, and sleep. Fatigue had lowered Elijah's guard.

Distraction — Martha from Luke 10:40. Martha was serving Jesus, yet the text says, "Martha was distracted with much serving." Her activity pulled her attention away from the very presence she was trying to honor. Distraction does not always come through sin; sometimes it comes through overactivity. That over-activity can be spiritual. I know a man who tries to do every prayer watch, go to church and watch every online Christian programming that there is. He can't of course; he is human with a human body.

False Security — Samson. Judges 16 Samson believed his strength would remain no matter what. After revealing the secret of his strength, Scripture says, "He awoke from his sleep and said, 'I will go out as at other times before and shake myself free. But he did not know that the LORD had left him. Samson assumed nothing had changed. False security left him exposed.

Deception. Eve in Genesis 3 The serpent did not begin with open rebellion. He began with subtle distortion: "Did God really say…?" Deception lowers the guard by altering perception. Eve was not attacked with force; she was persuaded through misrepresentation.

Gradual Compromise — Solomon in 1 Kings 11. Solomon did not fall in a single moment. Scripture says, "His wives turned his heart after other *gods*." The text describes slow drift. The wisest king in Israel allowed small compromises to accumulate until his heart was divided.

Emotional Turbulence — Peter, found in Luke 22. Peter confidently declared, "Lord, I am ready to go with You both to prison and to death." Yet within hours, under pressure and fear, he denied Jesus three times. Peter's guard fell under fear and emotional pressure.

Isolation — David Before the Census from 2 Samuel 24. David ordered a census of Israel against the warnings of Joab. Scripture implies a moment where David refused correction. Isolation from wise counsel allowed the decision to proceed. When leaders stop listening, their guard weakens.

Neglect / Laziness — David and Bathsheba, as seen in 2 Samuel 1. The passage begins with a very telling line:

> "In the spring, at the time when kings go out to battle… David remained at Jerusalem."

David was where he should not have been, doing what he should not have been doing. Neglect of responsibility created the conditions for temptation. His guard dropped long before he saw Bathsheba.

The guard rarely falls in dramatic fashion. In Scripture it often lowers quietly — through exhaustion, distraction, compromise, or neglect. These moments remind us that watchfulness is not a sign of fear, but of Wisdom.

NOT IN VAIN

Except the LORD keep the city, the watchman waketh but in vain. (Psalm 127:1)

This verse is often misunderstood. It does not say the watchman should not watch. The watchman still stands on the wall. The point is that watchfulness without God is empty, not that watchfulness is unnecessary.

So, the healthy Biblical balance is God watches. The watchman still stands his post. The Balance: Divine protection and human Watchfulness God protects. But God never commands people to abandon watchfulness.

The watchman on the wall cannot say, “God is protecting the city, so I will go to sleep.” Nor can the watchman say, “My watching alone will protect the city.”

Both are errors.

Scripture shows a partnership: God guards the city, and the watchman remains alert.

On the flip side, there are habits that open doors that should never be opened. If certain habits keep the enemy away, others quietly lower the guard. These often happen slowly and feel harmless at first.

Fatigue Without Recovery. Exhaustion weakens judgment. When people are depleted, overwhelmed, and running too hard, they often stop guarding important areas of life. Fatigue is one of the oldest ways vigilance collapses.

Distraction. Attention shifts away from what matters. Modern life multiplies distractions constant information, endless entertainment, emotional entanglements, new relationships that consume attention. When attention drifts, the guard is often lowered without noticing.

False Security. People assume danger cannot reach them. Examples include: familiarity, success, past victories, and trusted environments. Scripture repeatedly shows that danger often appears after confidence replaces caution.

Deception. Sometimes something looks good but isn't. Deception rarely appears as obvious evil. Instead it appears as reasonable, harmless, justified, and attractive. That's why discernment matters.

Compromise. Small permissions accumulate. Rarely does a life collapse from one dramatic decision. More often it is a small exception, a quiet rationalization, a tolerated habit. Over time those permissions weaken the guard.

Neglect. Some dangers arise not from rebellion but from simple neglect. People stop paying attention, examining their heart or correcting small misalignments. Neglect is subtle because nothing appears urgent.

Isolation. Correction disappears. Without wise voices nearby, people slowly lose perspective. Isolation often precedes major errors because no one is present to challenge wrong thinking.

Rebellion. Sometimes the guard is dropped deliberately. A person knows something is wrong but proceeds anyway. Rebellion is dangerous because it intentionally steps outside the protection that was already present.

Most doors are not broken open, they are simply left unguarded. God guards the city. But the watchman must still stand at the gate. Trust in God does not eliminate vigilance. It gives vigilance its purpose.

Without this balance people fall into two errors: Error 1. Passive Spirituality "God will handle everything." This produces negligence.

Error 2. Striving Spirituality "Everything depends on me." This produces anxiety. The right Biblical position is partnership. God protects, AND the Believer remains watchful. The watchman does not replace God. But neither does God replace the watchman. We guard with God, not instead of God. It is also not God, instead of man.

STRUCTURE AND THE GUARDED LIFE

A life that is guarded is rarely guarded by effort alone. It is guarded by **structure**. Structure is what keeps the roof on the house. When a house has walls, doors, gates, a roof, and watchmen, then entry becomes difficult. But when those things are missing, access becomes simple.

In many spiritual warfare descriptions, enemy forces speak of people whose lives are "open above." In simple terms, it means **there is no roof.** Without a roof, anything can enter. Nothing must ask permission, and the house offers no resistance. Rain enters. Wind enters. Debris enters. Witches enter, and evil entities have access.

This house is unguarded. Structure is missing.

Structure is not rigidity, nor is it legalism. It is simply the framework that protects what God has placed in a life. Examples of intangible structure might include boundaries, routines that strengthen the spirit, disciplined thinking, wise relationships, accountability, personal governance. Structure does not remove freedom. Structure **protects freedom**.

You are the house. Unguarded Houses -- When a life lacks structure, several things tend to happen. Decisions are reactive. Emotions govern choices. Impulses become normal. Boundaries dissolve. In effect, the house becomes easy to enter.

Not because the enemy is powerful. Because the house has **no roof**.

Unguarded hours often occur when structure temporarily collapses. When someone is tired, distracted, isolated, or overwhelmed. The routines and boundaries that normally protect them weaken.

That is when the "roof" becomes thin.

A guarded life is not built on intensity. It is built on structure. The watchman protects the gate, but structure protects the house.

Why does the enemy wait at the door? That is a tactic of war; attrition. Outlast the opponent. Evil entities are spiritual they have no physical body to maintain. Human bodies have limits. They get tired; they must rest. They can get emotional, and etcera.

Scripture answers that directly in several places. For example:

- 1 Peter 5:8 — the adversary as a roaring lion seeking someone to devour

- John 10:10 — the thief comes to steal, kill, and destroy
- Genesis 4:7 — sin crouching at the door

Scripture never portrays the enemy as merely wandering aimlessly. When the Bible describes him moving "to and fro" or prowling like a lion, it always connects that movement to purpose. The purpose is not mystery; the purpose of the crouching enemy is to harm or to seek advantage.

It is to steal, kill, or destroy.

To Steal - The first objective is often quiet theft. Things are taken slowly, sometimes unnoticed. Those things are intangible to man, but very real in the spirit realm: Peace, clarity, confidence, joy, focus, or even time. People may not realize anything has been stolen until much later.

To Kill - Not always physical life, but to kill something about or important to that life. Often what is targeted is something within a person. Hope, calling, courage, spiritual vitality. Relationships. Divine appointments or opportunities. The goal is to extinguish what God intended to live.

To Destroy. Destruction goes further than loss. It attempts to ruin or collapse what once functioned well such as families, reputations, faith, purpose, communities, ultimately, destiny. Where destruction succeeds, rebuilding becomes difficult.

The enemy waits. The enemy rarely attacks strongest structures head-on. Instead, he waits for moments when vigilance weakens fatigue, distraction, resentment, pride, and isolation.

These are the **unguarded hours**.

The lion does not roar constantly. Often, he waits quietly until the moment is right.

The enemy rarely forces entry. He prefers doors that are already unattended. That is taken as invitation or permission.

This is why Scripture repeatedly calls for watchfulness. Not because believers live in fear, but because something real moves through the world looking for access. The watchman does not stand on the wall because danger is certain. He stands there because danger is possible.

THREE THREATS AND THE STRONGEST PROTECTIONS

If the enemy steals, kills, and destroys — what protects a life?

Jesus summarized the enemy's agenda clearly in John 10:10. *The thief cometh not, but for to steal, and to kill, and to destroy.* Each of those has a corresponding protection.

Protection Against Theft *(things being stolen from a life).* The strongest protection against theft in Scripture is watchfulness joined with stewardship. Watchfulness**.** Jesus repeatedly commanded vigilance:

Watch therefore: for ye know not what hour your Lord doth come. (Matthew 24:42)

Watchfulness means paying attention, guarding what has been entrusted, and not assuming everything will remain safe automatically.

It means stewardship. What God gives must be actively kept. Adam was placed in the garden not only to enjoy it but to keep it (Genesis 2:15). To keep something means to guard it, to maintain it, to refuse access to what harms it. The enemy steals most easily from what people stop guarding.

Protection Against Things Being Killed *(hope, calling, faith, relationships, purpose).* The strongest protection for a life is connection to God and His Word.

He that abideth in me, and I in him, the same bringeth forth much fruit. (John 15:5)

Abiding keeps life flowing. Things tend to die when they become disconnected from their source. That includes faith, spiritual vitality, clarity of calling.

Abiding involves remaining close to God, remaining rooted in truth, and refusing to drift away from life-giving sources. When life remains connected to God, what is meant to live is far harder to extinguish.

Protection Against Destruction *(collapse, ruin, annihilation).* The strongest protection against destruction is structure built on Truth. Jesus described this clearly in Matthew 7:24-25. The wise man built his house upon a rock. When storms came rain fell, floods rose, winds beat against the house. But the house did not fall because the foundation was solid.

Structure includes obedience to Truth, disciplined thinking, wise boundaries, and stability of character. Destruction most often occurs when a life is built without a foundation.

Threat	**Protection Summary:**
Steal	Watchfulness and stewardship
Kill	Abiding in the source of life
Destroy	Structure built on Truth

The enemy's intentions are simple: steal, kill, and destroy. The protections God gives are also simple: watchfulness, life in Him, and a life built on Truth. What God entrusts must be guarded. What God gives life must remain connected to Him. What God builds must stand on Truth.

YOU ARE A CITY

The Bible repeatedly treats human life like a city with gates. If the gates are guarded, the city stands. If the gates are neglected, access becomes easy.

He that hath no rule over his own spirit is like a city that is broken down, and without walls. (Proverbs 25:28)

Entry and access points matter greatly. A man's gates require careful watch. The Three Gates That Must Be Guarded

The Eye Gate. *(What a person allows themselves to look at).* What enters through the eyes shapes thoughts, desires, and imagination.

Jesus spoke about this::

The light of the body is the eye… if thine eye be evil, thy whole body shall be full of darkness. (Matthew 6:22-23)

When the eye gate is unguarded comparison grows, temptation multiplies, desire is inflamed, and discernment dulls. When it is guarded clarity increases, discipline strengthens, and the mind remains steadier. A guarded life pays attention to what it continually looks at and is not lackadaisical about it.

The Ear Gate. *(What a person allows themselves to hear and absorb).* Words shape perception more than people realize. Proverbs repeatedly emphasizes the importance of guarding what one listens to. For example, Proverbs 4:20 urges attentiveness to wise instruction.

When the ear gate is unguarded lies gain influence, gossip reshapes thinking, fear spreads easily, and bitterness grows. But when the ear gate is guarded, Truth has space to settle. Wisdom can take root, and discernment strengthens. People become what they **continually listen to**.

The Heart Gate. *(The inner life where decisions and loyalties form).* This is the most important gate. Scripture makes that abundantly obvious:

Keep thy heart with all diligence; for out of it are the issues of life. (Proverbs 4:23)

The heart determines motives, decisions, loyalties, and direction. If the heart becomes corrupted, every other part of life eventually follows. Guarding the heart involves examining your own motives, rejecting bitterness, refusing pride, and keeping affection oriented toward what is good.

Cities in the ancient world were not protected by watching **every inch of wall**. They guarded the **gates**. Cities automatically had gates; God never told anyone to go build a gate, but we are instructed to guard our own gates. We are also promised that we will possess the gates of our enemies. Gates are where entry happens.

The same is true of a life.

Most problems do not appear out of nowhere. They enter through places that were **left open**. A guarded life does not attempt to control everything. It simply guards the gates. When the gates are watched, the city rests safely.

Unguarded hours are often the moments when these gates are left unattended. Times when the mind drifts or when emotions rule, or when attention fades. That is when access becomes easiest.

Baby Gates. Sometimes protection is very simple. Anyone who has raised small children knows about baby gates. They are placed at stairways or doorways to prevent a child from wandering into danger. The purpose is not punishment, it is there for safety, not to restrict freedom unnecessarily. The baby gate is there because a child does not yet understand where danger lies.

Most parents know they should install the gate. Many even purchase one. But sometimes the gate is left leaning against the wall. Sometimes it is never installed. Sometimes the adult thinks:

"It will be fine."
"I'll watch closely."
"It's only for a minute."

Kids are quick; they move fast. Many times faster than expected. They could get hurt or get into trouble.

The problem was never the absence of a gate. The problem was the **uninstalled gate**.

The Same Principle Applies to Life. Many of the protections God gives people function like gates. They are simple safeguards boundaries, routines, wise counsel, and disciplines that keep a life stable. None of these things are complicated, but they must be **put in place and implemented.** A gate leaning against the wall protects no one.

A derelict watchman leaning on a wall, possibly even sleeping protects no one.

Many lives are injured not because protection was unavailable, but because the gate was never put in place. An uninstalled gate guards nothing. If you are the watchman of your house, are you doing your job?

Adults must guard **their own gates**. Parents must also guard the gates of those **who cannot yet guard themselves**.

A toddler can't watch himself or watch out for himself. The parent must guard them. So, the gate is placed there as protection until the child grows old enough to recognize risk and govern themselves. If there is a gate; there is a watchman; that is understood.

Something important happens when a person becomes responsible for a child. The parent must now guard **two lives instead of one**. They must guard their own gates, **and** the gates of the child entrusted to them. Children learn safety from the structure surrounding them.

One of the marks of maturity is learning to guard one's own gates. A child may not yet know what to listen to what to look at what influences are harmful. But an adult must learn and know these things. If adults refuse to guard their own gates, the children under their care often inherit the consequences.

Baby gates are temporary. They are not meant to remain forever. They exist until the child becomes capable of recognizing danger and exercising judgment. In the same way, spiritual maturity involves moving from being protected by others to **governing oneself**. A mature life does not depend entirely on someone else standing watch. It learns to stand watch.

Children cannot guard their own gates. That responsibility belongs to the adults entrusted with them—until the day the child grows into a watchman of their own life. A child is protected by the structure surrounding them. An adult must become part of that structure. Know that the structure is not only physical; these gates that need guarding are spiritual.

MODERN SITUATIONS WHERE THE GUARD DROPS

1. Fatigue

A person begins spending time with a new group of friends who stay out late, travel often, and keep a fast pace of activity. Wanting to belong, they keep up with the schedule. Sleep becomes irregular. Quiet time disappears. Discernment grows dull. Nothing dramatic has happened, but exhaustion has quietly weakened watchfulness.

2. Distraction. A new romantic relationship begins. Conversations stretch late into the night. Time once spent in prayer or reflection is replaced by constant messaging and phone calls. Attention shifts completely toward the relationship. The person has not abandoned faith—but **their focus has been captured**.

3. False Security

Someone has been stable in their life and faith for many years. Because nothing difficult has happened recently, they assume: "Nothing will happen to me." Spiritual attentiveness fades because life feels predictable. Confidence quietly becomes **carelessness**.

Unguarded With the Girls John 3:27 John answered and said, A man can receive nothing, except it be given him from Heaven.

1 Corinthians 4:7

Genesis 34:1-2 Now Dinah the daughter of Leah, whom she had borne to Jacob, went out (Unescorted) to visit the girls of the land…

The gods are calling, always calling – when you go by yourself, you could be taken by the prince of Shechem and attacked

4. Deception

A work opportunity appears extremely attractive. It promises more money, recognition influence. Yet something about the environment feels unsettled. Instead of pausing to examine it, the person accepts quickly, trusting the promise of advancement. The guard lowered because **the opportunity looked good**.

5. Gradual Compromise. A person begins allowing small things they once resisted. A conversation that crosses boundaries. Entertainment that slowly reshapes values. A habit that once seemed harmless. None of it seems serious on its own. But over time, small allowances accumulate until discernment grows weaker.

6. Emotional Turbulence. Someone experiences a painful disappointment—perhaps betrayal, loss, or sudden conflict. In the rush of emotion they say things they later regret, make decisions quickly, withdraw from wise counsel. Strong emotion narrowed their perspective. The guard dropped because **the moment felt overwhelming**.

7. Isolation. A person moves to a new city or begins working remotely. Gradually they lose connection with trusted voices who once spoke into their life. Without realizing it, they begin making decisions alone. Perspective narrows because **no one else sees what they are seeing**.

8. Neglect / Laziness. Life becomes busy and comfortable. Prayer is postponed. Scripture reading becomes occasional. Reflection is replaced by entertainment. Nothing seems urgent enough to maintain discipline. Slow neglect quietly lowers vigilance.

9. Rebellion. A person receives wise counsel from family, mentors, or spiritual leadership but begins to resent the boundaries being placed around them. They decide, "I will do what I want." The guard drops because they **step outside the protection that came with guidance**.

When they step out from God's Word, they lose protection. **Example: Korah's Rebellion**

Numbers 16

Korah and others challenged the authority God had established through Moses and Aaron.

They declared:

“You take too much upon yourselves… the whole congregation is holy.”

Their rebellion was not confusion.
It was **defiance of the structure God had put in place**.

By stepping outside that order, they stepped outside the protection that came with it.

Rebellion is not simply disagreement.
It is **rejecting rightful authority in order to claim it for oneself**.

10. Disobedience. Someone knows clearly what God has already made right or wrong in their life. Yet in a moment of pressure or desire they say, “Just this once.”

Disobedience rarely begins with confusion. It begins with **ignoring what is already known**. **Example: King Saul and the Amalekites**

1 Samuel 15

Saul was given a clear instruction regarding the Amalekites.

Instead, he spared King Agag and kept the best livestock.

When confronted, Saul justified his actions:

“I have obeyed the LORD.”

But Samuel answered:

“To obey is better than sacrifice.”

Saul’s guard did not fall because he lacked knowledge.

It fell because he **substituted his judgment for God's command**.

Disobedience weakens protection because it **breaks alignment**.

11. Willful Acts of the Flesh A person pursues immediate gratification even when they understand the long-term cost. Perhaps financial recklessness, destructive relationships, addiction to pleasure or escape

The moment feels satisfying. But the decision trades **inheritance for appetite**.

11. Willful Acts of the Flesh

Sometimes the guard drops because a person knowingly chooses **desire over discipline**.

Example: Esau Selling His Birthright

Genesis 25

Esau returned from the field hungry and asked Jacob for food.

Jacob replied that Esau must sell his birthright.

Scripture says:

"Thus Esau despised his birthright."

The decision was not forced.

It was a moment where **immediate appetite overruled long-term inheritance**.

Willful indulgence can cause a person to surrender what once protected them.

Or negligence, laziness. Dry Christianity.

Willful acts: A person may not decide to be jealous, but they decide to stay jealous if they don't fight it. If they don't repent of it and resist that green eyed devil.

Dating

I've met so many men that are jealous of me. I'm not trying to be a man, never have tried to be one. I am a prissy, girly-girl. I'm practical, though, but most disappointment I've had in dating or marriage is when I finally come to realize or am willing to admit that a grown man who is supposed to be my protector, my spiritual covering, my friend and lover is jealous of me.

Jealousy and love can never walk together. Jealousy is a work of the flesh and if you are jealous OF someone you will never love them.

If you have jealousy in your heart, will you ever LOVE anyone.

Satan is jealous. Envious. Covetous. He said that he would exalt his throne--, his own throne.

God's name is Jealous because He is jealous OVER us, very protective. But He is also jealous as He will not tolerate idolatry. If we are to be married to the Lamb, then prophetically and by faith we already are… Jesus is my husband, I will have no other *gods*, not just before Him, but shouldn't it stand to reason that we have no other *gods*, amen?

Cain was jealous of Abel, then killed him.

Saul was jealous of David, hunted him like a dog to kill him.

Jacob's boys were jealous of Joseph, wanted to kill him, but instead faked his death and sold him into slavery. The son of a prince, sold as a common slave.

Jesus, the son of the King, Himself the Prince of Peace, sold for the price of a slave by Judas.

Jealousy in someone close or someone proximal historically has been the most dangerous thing of all.

ALIENATION

Yeah, but **while** you sinned you were being ripped off. Sin causes alienation from God – while you are out of God's sight – because you hid, or think you hid in order to commit sin – you were unprotected, unguarded – ripe for spoilage. The devil can do what he likes to you. And what does he like? He likes to steal, kill, and destroy.

You're supposed to be the **Bride** of Christ, so don't allow yourself to be *groomed.* You are the Bride.

What is the enemy doing? When you are alone, left alone, unattended, or have chosen to leave the coverage area—that is, into sin, disobedience, rebellion, ignoring quenching, or grieving the Holy Spirit.

More examples follow in the next chapters.

THE WATCHMAN IS *OWNED*

12. **When the Watchman is Owned.** A compromised watchman who still occupies the post is worse than having no watchman at all, because people believe they are protected. A city without a watchman is vulnerable. But a city with a compromised watchman is in even greater danger. The watchman still stands on the wall. He still carries the appearance of authority. He still occupies the position, but something has changed.

His vigilance is gone.

The appearance remains. From the outside, nothing looks different. The watchman still looks like the watchman. He still speaks like the watchman. He still holds the post assigned to him. Those inside the city believe someone is watching. They assume the gates are being guarded. They trust the structure because the structure appears intact.

Appearances can deceive.

When the Watchman is owned. Sometimes a watchman is not merely tired or distracted. Sometimes he has been compromised. He may be bribed, manipulated, deceived, intimidated and entangled in something that now controls him.

He still believes he is standing watch. (Because he thinks no one knows – not even God?) Others still believe he is protecting the city. But the enemy no longer needs to scale the wall. The gatekeeper has already been neutralized.

This condition is dangerous because it is invisible. People inside the city sleep peacefully. They assume someone is alert. They assume the gate is guarded. They assume the watchman is faithful. But the city is no longer protected. Not because the walls fell. Because the watchman did.

Scripture warns about this. The Bible repeatedly warns about leaders, watchmen, and shepherds who fail to guard what was entrusted to them.

> But if the watchman see the sword come, and blow not the trumpet, and the people be not warned… his blood will I require at the watchman's hand. (Ezekiel 33:6):

The watchman's role is not symbolic; it is real responsibility.

The city is safest when the watchman is faithful. But the city is most vulnerable when the watchman is compromised. A sleeping watchman is dangerous. A compromised watchman is catastrophic. Sometimes the one assigned to guard **everyone else** has become compromised. And no one knows.

a passage in Isaiah where God describes watchmen who **cannot bark or warn**.

His watchmen are blind: they are all ignorant, they are all dumb dogs, they cannot bark; sleeping, lying down, loving to slumber. (Isaiah 56:10)

That's a very important question—and a serious one. When people depend on someone in a watchman-like role (a leader, guardian, advisor, or anyone entrusted with warning and care), it can be hard to know if that person has become compromised before harm occurs. Scripture and practical wisdom both suggest that the safest approach is not to rely on a single person unquestioningly but to cultivate shared vigilance and accountability.

Here are some principles that help people discern whether a watchman is still trustworthy:

Look for accountability, not isolation. Healthy watchmen are not above correction. They welcome counsel and transparency.

- Proverbs 11:14 teaches that safety comes from many advisers.
- If someone refuses oversight, shuts down questions, or avoids peers who can challenge them, that's a warning sign.

Shared responsibility reduces the risk that one compromised person can quietly endanger everyone else.

Examine the fruit over time. Jesus emphasized evaluating leaders by the results of their lives:

- Matthew 7:16 — *"You will know them by their fruits."*

Consistent patterns—integrity, humility, care for others—build trust. Patterns of secrecy, manipulation, or self-interest erode it.

Notice whether warnings are being given. A faithful watchman alerts people to real dangers. Silence or minimization when problems are evident can indicate trouble. The role itself involves vigilance and timely warning.

- Ezekiel 33:6 describes a watchman who fails to warn when danger approaches.

Compare words with Truth. People should measure teaching or guidance against trusted standards.

- Acts 17:11 praises those who examined teachings carefully instead of accepting them blindly.

Independent verification protects against misplaced trust.

Keep personal discernment active. Even when someone holds a leadership role, individuals remain responsible for their own alertness.

- 1 Peter 5:8 urges believers themselves to be sober and watchful.

A community where everyone maintains awareness is much safer than one that assumes a single person will guard everything.

A trustworthy watchman does not replace the vigilance of others. Instead, they strengthen it.

When people rely entirely on one individual without shared discernment or accountability, the system becomes fragile. But when vigilance is distributed—supported by truth, transparency, and community—the risk of hidden compromise drops dramatically.

A faithful watchman strengthens the vigilance of the people. A compromised one discourages it. The safest city is the one where everyone remains awake, but since that is not possible, then someone is always awake and that or those someone's should be watchmen.

A watchman is not just anyone. This watch over the city, the house, the family, the man himself needs to see, hear and discern in the spirit. Else there may not be enough notice to properly act before trouble, trauma or disaster.

FAMILIARITY

13. Discernment Overridden by Loyalty Pressure. People sometimes feel something is wrong, but repeated messaging from family or authority figures teaches them to dismiss their own perception. Discernment can be trained out of someone, overridden by Familiarity Sometimes the guard drops not because a person fails to notice something wrong, but because they have been taught to ignore what they notice.

A child or young adult may sense that a relative's behavior is troubling or manipulative. Yet they hear the same response repeatedly:

"That's your brother."
"That's your cousin."
"Play nice."
"You're family."

Over time, the message becomes clear: loyalty is more important than discernment. The person is forced to learn to silence their instincts. Ironically, outsiders may see the problem immediately. They are not influenced by family expectations or emotional obligation. But the individual inside the family may struggle to acknowledge what is plainly visible.

This does not always come from malicious parents or relatives. Sometimes it comes from well-meaning adults who simply want peace in the family and discourage conflict, even if the conflict brings real Peace and not the fake kind. But when discernment is repeatedly dismissed, the inner guard weakens.

He that loveth father or mother more than me is not worthy of me: and he that loveth son or daughter more than me is not worthy of me. (Matthew 10:37)

A guarded life requires learning that recognizing harmful behavior is not disloyalty. It is Wisdom. This is a hard line to draw. God is talking in any of the ways He speaks, but you are instead listening to your mother, father, sister, brother, other relative or person instead of God. This is a problem. The guard drops from pressure to ignore one's own perception.

It's you relative; you let down your guard. It's your friend; you let down your guard. It's your co-worker – okay you've learned by now; do not let down your guard. Being in the flesh doesn't mean at the moment that you are supposed to be watching or guarding your vessel, your house, family, ministry, business or career. You cannot be entangled in the flesh over here and then when you get home you are now the priest, prophet, and pastor of the home.

Repeatedly. Regularly. Without repentance. It doesn't work like that. What you do at the club or wherever does affect your home and all of your life. Iniquity is sticky, it follows folks wherever they go.

Familiarity lowers the guard. That's why the devil sends a familiar spirit to people to get information out of them or really to fake-befriend them and lead them along the pathways to hell. A monitoring spirit is sent to watch, gather information and report back. That familiar spirit talks. People think they are talking to all kinds of folks: dead relatives, ancestors, deceased celebrities, almost anyone that you can think up, have thought obsessively about, grieved over, or fantasized about. These are familiar spirits, not your dearly departed granny.

Watchman, or supposed to be watchman the more you let down your discernment and guard and talk to or entertain these 'beings" like strays, the longer they will stay around and embed themselves into your life. Eventually a person could be led into all error.

Familiarity lowers the guard. Perhaps this person is your relative or someone you know well, even someone who knows someone you know--, sometimes that's enough. Somehow, some where trust has been established so familiar voices or names feel safe. But are they? They must be discerned; just because they feel safe does not mean they shouldn't be examined.

What Jesus says in Matthew 10:37 is not an attack on or a rejection of family but it is a correction of spiritual priority. Love, especially human love must never replace alignment. Because when love replaces alignment, discernment is often set aside.

Trusted Voices can be so dangerous. People do not usually abandon discernment for strangers--, not usually. But they do they abandon it for people they trust. That includes family, leaders, mentors, and authority figures from all aspects of their life. When a trusted voice speaks, people often stop checking, stop discerning, and stop listening inwardly. They assume, "If they said it, it must be right, or it must be so."

Scripture never instructs a person to follow another human voice **instead of God**. The shift is rarely dramatic; it's subtle. Remember, the serpent is more *subtile* than the other animals in the Garden, (Genesis).

Familiarity creates unguarded moments. One's guard is not dropped in fear; it is dropped in comfort. The person is not trying to do wrong; they simply stop watching. This also happens when people go into familiar places even if they don't know the people there. Work. Church. Their regular gym, and etcetera.

Sometimes the familiar isn't human at all. Not their voice, not their sound, not their looks or words. In dreams there are masquerades all the time. Something may not even be human but it masquerading as human and often as someone you know and trust. This is how some end up having sex in the dream; they think it is their spouse, or their partner or some hot person they're interested in. It's a demon.

These entities can also copy voices and voice patterns. A person doesn't even have to be asleep to hear an evil call. If you hear your name, do not answer unless you know that you know that you know it's the Holy Spirit. If you answer the fist time to an evil call they will keep talking. They may suggest to you or instruct you to do things you would NEVER think of doing.

Discernment: When you open any gate to let in something illegal—baby, the gate is open. It is simply open and you did it. When you answer and listen to a demon, you just opened a spiritual door that will be harder to close than it was to open, when you finally realize that it was opened.

This is especially dangerous because like those phishing phone calls what you say on the first call can entrap you. The thing in these spiritual matters though is you may hear your name, if you answer, there may be an evil instruction following, but you don't even hear the instruction. But it still happened, and it's like a programming. Pray. Do not answer unless you are positive it is the Lord. If you discern that it is not, speak out loud and demand it stop, go away, and announce that you will not follow any instructions given whether you heard any words after your name or not.

The watchman does not leave his post just because the voice sounds familiar. The watchman doesn't do counter to what the Lord says, ever, no matter who is speaking or who they think is speaking.

SPF – SPIRITUAL PROTECTIVE FORCE

God does not tell us to watch and pray just to give us something to do, or make us busy. When we don't watch and pray we are *unguarded*. Yes, God gives His angels charge over us to keep us in all our ways, but they respond to the voice of the Word of God. If we are not speaking it, then the angel's assignments are nebulous or non-existent.

Pray, ask the Lord for protection; ask Him to give His angels charge over you, daily. Now if we are counting on someone else to do it for us – really? They have to watch and pray for themselves, their own stuff, the stuff they have stewardship over, their own spouse, family, children, house, cars, bank account – their own intangibles—virtues, honor, position. YOU cover your own, or in unguarded hours you may be ripped off. Here, it becomes obvious that we need one another because we are humans, in flesh, we must sleep at some point, so none of us can watch and pray 24 hours a day.

How long does a prayer last? Prayers extend past time and space, but if a watch is 3 hours, I would say that at the most, 3 hours from your last prayer, you might consider praying again. The Bible says to pray without ceasing. You'd apply sunblock with an SPF of 30 every half hour, right? SPF 90, every 90 minutes, right? Most people eat or feed their babies every 4 hours. Some things are done and repeated, it is called diligence.

Therefore, one should either pray without ceasing, or at least once per watch, with is every three hours. Pray with all diligence.

My soul sinneth against Thee – my God of Mercy. Sin doesn't just *happen.* Sin takes invitation, planning, evil escort, and an evil *anointing.* Sin involves your whole being, your soul – whether you think it's your body (he sinneth against his own body) it is because a body is used in the sin, but emotions are enticed, intellect -how to do it, where to do it, how to get away with it. .. because the sinner man, the carnal man, with appetite who is lusting for *experiences* ever thinks he will outsmart God.

Well, the devil may present that to man as, enjoy yourself, *live a little.* Really, he is encouraging or convincing man that he can outsmart sin. But sin has iniquity. As said before iniquity is sticky; it sticks to a man. Sin has consequences.

So, how does one outsmart the *consequences* of sin?

He doesn't. Can you walk through rain without getting wet? Can you sit in a sauna without getting hot? Or walk through snow, barefoot without getting cold?

Can a man take fire in his bosom and not get burned? Sin is fire.

Sure, you can speed in your car and feel that you got away with it. The devil gives you another *fun* thing to do and may provide the anointing for you to temporarily get away with it --, in the natural. This is akin to beginner's luck in gambling. That's the hook. Don't fall for that, please.

Then, the next thing, and the next, so now in the natural you have been *groomed* to think you are smarter or can get away with things that other people get caught doing. At the time it is happening a person can be so hyped to feel that now they are a master driver, a speedster, quick, agile, and really smart. They want to become a NASCAR driver now. The devil has groomed this person and made that person intoxicated, high on their recklessness, their lawlessness.

Man is ever ignoring TIME. The law will catch up to the criminal. The Law of Sin and Death will catch up to the sinner. Time will catch all. So, whatever we may think we got away with, it is stored in Time. Don't ignore Time.

You may never be stopped by a traffic cop for road violations, and you may think that you're okay to do anything you want on the road and in your car--, well, at least you think that regarding speeding, until a traffic ticket comes in the mail, next month.

The soul that sinneth shall surely die. My soul has sinned against thee; Lord forgive me so that what has been deposited or installed in my soul doesn't kill me, either suddenly, or slowly, in the Name of Jesus. *Amen.*

UNGUARDED HOURS EXIST

There are hours in every life when vigilance drops—not because of rebellion, but because of humanity. Fatigue lowers attention. Familiarity softens caution. Trust quiets suspicion. Routine creates autopilot. Or you just think no one is watching, I'll do what I please.

And sleep, which God Himself ordained, suspends conscious awareness altogether. These are not moral failures. They are design features.

Yet design features create conditions.

There are hours when people are less guarded—not reckless, not careless, simply **less defended**. These hours occur late at night, early in the morning, during grief, during transition, during sustained pressure, during illness, during caregiving, during distractions, during times of relaxation and fellowship, and during seasons of prolonged responsibility.

Scripture does not deny the existence of such hours. It names them.

"While men slept…" "Watch and pray…" "The spirit indeed is willing, but the flesh is weak…" The Bible never assumes uninterrupted human alertness. It assumes limitation—and then addresses what must be done because of it.

The problem is not that unguarded hours exist. The problem is pretending they do not.

Unguarded does not mean a person is unfaithful, it is important to say plainly: unguarded hours are not evidence of spiritual laziness. Unguarded hours actually often arrive after obedience, after endurance, after a fast, after a marathon prayer, restraint, and after faithfulness.

They say the first step of a long journey is the hardest, but many people encounter their most vulnerable at the point of exhaustion. When they have done everything they know to do and no longer have strength to maintain conscious vigilance.

This book is not written to accuse such people. It is written to tell the truth about what those hours require.

There is an overlap that no one likes to discuss but it is there. I don't mean to go all *science-y* on you but Psychology acknowledges that exhaustion impairs judgment, slows reaction time, and weakens executive control. Scripture acknowledges that there is an adversary who seeks opportunity, not permission. These two realities overlap. The spiritual realm does not pause because the human body must rest. That is not cause for fear—but it is cause for Wisdom.

Unguarded hours are not dangerous because people sleep. They are dangerous when nothing has been intentionally ordered to stand watch when they do.

We have not been left without comfort. We have not been left without help, but God has equipped and blessed us to be self-sustaining

As a teenager, I watched this play out in a way that stayed with me. A friend—an only child—was given everything. Not spoiled in the dramatic sense, just oddly disengaged. For her sixteenth birthday, her parents gave her a brand-new sports car. It was stunning. Everyone wanted it. Everyone would have treasured it.

One day in high school, a group of us skipped school and went to the mall—that was when the mall was cool, and we all thought we were too. After lunch, she said she was tired, handed me the keys, climbed into the back seat, and went to sleep.

She didn't resent the car. She didn't reject it. She simply didn't care to drive it. That moment taught me something I didn't yet have language for. That day I saw that a gift can be possessed without being appreciated, stewarded or used. Something valuable can be entrusted to you and still go unused—not because it lacks worth, but because you refuse the responsibility of engaging it.

When we have responsibility and ability to be the watchman in our lives or in others and we don't do it, when we have discernment, but don't use it, that is the same as not appreciating gifts from God.

NIGHT HOURS OF THE SOUL

The night hours are not about when a man is literally sleeping. Night seasons are when clarity fades, answers are not obvious, strength feels reduced, or vigilance must continue anyway.

The spirit remains attentive even when the body must rest; the spirit does not sleep. Every life eventually passes through seasons that feel like night.

This is the kind of darkness that comes when strength is low and answers are not obvious. The mind grows tired, the heart grows heavy, and the usual clarity that guides decisions feels distant. These are the night hours of the soul. Night hours do not necessarily mean something is wrong. In Scripture, many faithful people walked through periods where they could not see clearly ahead.

David spoke about walking through the valley of deep shadow in Psalm 23:4. Paul described seasons of pressure beyond what seemed bearable in 2 Corinthians 1:8. These moments come to nearly everyone.

What matters now is how a person lives during them.

Night hours of the soul are dangerous, not because God is absent, but it is when **vigilance weakens**. When people are tired or discouraged, they often lower their guard, stop examining their thoughts, and make decisions simply to relieve pressure. The enemy does not need dramatic opportunities. He often waits for moments when a person is simply exhausted.

That is when watchfulness becomes most difficult—and most necessary.

A watchman stands his post precisely because night exists. If everything were bright and obvious, a watchman would not be necessary. But darkness hides movement and disguises danger. The watchman exists for the hours when others cannot see clearly. In the same way, spiritual vigilance matters most during the quiet seasons when certainty fades and fatigue grows.

During these night seasons, dramatic physical human effort is rarely what protects a person. Instead, the quiet disciplines of a guarded life become essential. staying close to Truth, refusing impulsive decisions, maintaining structure even when emotions fluctuate, remembering what God has already made clear. In other words, the watchman remains at the gate.

Night hours do not last forever. Morning eventually arrives. But the condition of a life at daybreak often depends on what happened while the world was dark. Some lives emerge from the night strengthened. Others suffer damage that began in the quiet hours when vigilance faded. The difference is often very simple. Someone remained on watch.

Loss is rarely in one reckless moment; it is usually slowly — in unguarded hours.

WHEN THE WATCHMAN IS TIRED

Not all distraction is by fatigue, or the lowering of defenses. Not all distraction is chosen. Some distraction is pursued—entertainment, avoidance, overstimulation, numbing. Some distraction is imposed—grief, caregiving, crisis, overload, long obedience without relief.

Both have the same effect.

Attention narrows. Awareness dulls. Reaction slows. And the mind, overwhelmed or exhausted, begins to release what it cannot actively manage. This is not sin. This is saturation.

Vigilance can become hypervigilance and that can make a person delirious or near loco. Hyper-vigilance can easily become unsustainable. There are seasons when staying alert requires more strength than is humanly available. People describe it in different ways.

- “I can’t think straight anymore.”
- “I don’t even look like myself.”
- “I don’t trust what happens if I stop.”

- “I’m afraid to sleep, but I can’t stay awake.”

These are not the words of rebellion. They are the words of people who have been **on watch too long**. At this point, one of two errors usually follows:

1. **Hypervigilance** – refusing rest, leading to collapse
2. **Resignation** – disengaging without order, leading to vulnerability

Neither is Wisdom.

Scripture offers a third way: delegation. Delegation is not surrender. There are times when the body must rest, but responsibility must not lapse. Wise people delegate.

Parents give instructions before leaving. Leaders assign watches. Commanders issue orders before nightfall. The existence of delegation does not imply abandonment. It implies order.

The question is not whether the body will sleep. The question is whether anything or anyone has been instructed to stand watch when it does.

Now, just because you’re tired or exhausted don’t be negligent. Don't sell your birthright just because you're hungry like Esau who got someone to do for him that which he probably could do for himself.

Don't just fall asleep 'hoping' just because you’re exhausted; don't give up just because you're human and so tired. You have divine resources; your spirit man is one of those divine resources with access to more divine help.

Being human explains vulnerability. Being human does not excuse abdication. Exhaustion is real, but it is not permission to forfeit inheritance. Hunger does not justify bad exchange. Fatigue does not cancel discernment. Rest is allowed; surrender is not.

In other words, human limitation calls for Wisdom, not stupidity. That is not cruel. That is *adult*.

Esau? He wasn't really wicked in that moment. He was hungry, tired, and impulsive. He did not lose his birthright because he hated it. He lost it because he valued immediate relief over long-term authority. Do not trade spiritual authority for temporary relief just because you are exhausted.

Being human does not mean being careless. Scripture never treats exhaustion as permission to make foolish exchanges. Esau did not sell his birthright because he was evil, but because he was hungry—and unwilling to govern himself in that moment. Fatigue explains vulnerability, but it does not excuse abdication. Do not fall asleep hoping simply because you are tired. Do not surrender what carries authority just because relief is immediate. You have Divine resources available to you, and wisdom uses them—especially when the body is weak.

The answer is not to deny your humanity, but to steward it. God has not left you without resources simply because you are tired. The regenerated inner man is one of those resources—alive to God, capable of discernment, and able to remain aligned with the Holy Spirit when the body must rest. Human weakness does not eliminate divine help. It makes its proper use necessary.

Human limitation does not cancel Divine provision. It demands its wise use.

When the answer is not, “Try harder.” It is not to force yourself to “Stay awake.” “Push through. “No, the answer is “Do not make permanent losses because of temporary weakness.” Instead, we must learn to set order to what must be ordered. We must learn to rest without forfeiting authority. That is not severity that is stewardship.

A lot of people want to get someone else to do their spiritual stuff for them, they are abdicating. Even if you get someone else to do something for you, there is no guarantee that someone else is actually doing what they say--, even spiritual things. A real minister in Africa laughed one day and said to me regarding other people they have met, "If they tell you they are going up to the 'mountain' (on someone's behalf), they are really at home watching Netflix."

Worse, I’ve met people who will feign to “cover” another in ministry when they, themselves are not even in right standing with the Lord. I’m not judging anyone, I’ve judging authority and if they have the right authority to cover me, for example either as a pastor, or to cover me in any aspect of ministry that I may need covering for.

Scripture never teaches blind delegation—only *wise* delegation. Try every *spirit* and you will know them by their fruit. In order to have Godly fruit, one needs to be connected to the Spirit of God.

RESTORE the GUARD

Next we discuss how the guard returns once it has dropped. The guard does not return through panic or self-condemnation. The guard is restored through **reorientation and realignment.**

A guarded life is not sustained by fear. It is sustained by clarity and alignment.

Pause.

When the guard has dropped, the first step is not action. It is stopping.

Pausing breaks the momentum of reacting or overreacting. It breaks the momentum of emotional escalation, impulsive decisions. A person cannot regain watchfulness while still rushing forward. Sometimes restoration begins with simply standing still long enough to see clearly again.

Return to Truth. Confusion weakens the guard; Truth restores it. Returning to truth may involve revisiting Scripture, recalling what God has already made clear, rejecting thoughts that distort reality.

Truth re-establishes **orientation**.

Reclaim Attention. Distraction is one of the main reasons the guard falls. Restoration requires directing attention back where it belongs. This means deliberately stepping away from unnecessary noise, constant commentary, and emotional agitation. Attention must be gathered again.

Strengthen the Interior Life. The guard is strongest when the inner life is steady. This happens through prayer, quiet reflection, listening rather than reacting, and allowing your own spirit to settle and be aligned with the Holy Spirit of God. Watchfulness grows naturally when the inner life becomes ordered again.

Accept Limits. Exhaustion weakens vigilance. Sometimes restoring the guard requires something very simple: **Rest**. This may mean sleep, stepping away from pressure, and allowing the body to recover. A person who refuses limits cannot remain watchful for long.

Seek Wise Perspective. At times the guard is restored through the perspective of others. Trusted voices can help reveal what we cannot see alone.

Not every opinion should be heard, but wise counsel can clarify confusion, challenge assumptions, bring balance

Guarding is strengthened when discernment is shared.

Resume Quiet Discipline. Once clarity returns, the guard is maintained through ordinary discipline. This includes governing thoughts, maintaining watchfulness, and refusing unnecessary compromise

Guarding is not dramatic; it is **steady**.

When the guard has dropped, restoration does not require force. It requires returning to clarity, stillness, and truth. Watchfulness grows again when a person reclaims attention and realigns with what is already known.

WHAT A GUARDED LIFE LOOKS LIKE

Guarding does not mean living in suspicion or fear. It means living with awareness, alignment, and restraint. A guarded life is marked by several quiet characteristics.

Watchfulness. A guarded person pays attention. They notice shifts in atmosphere. changes in thought patterns. pressures that influence decisions. Watchfulness keeps the inner life awake.

Discipline. Guarding requires consistent habits. This includes governing thoughts, managing time, refusing unnecessary compromise. Discipline protects what is valuable over the long term.

Humility. A guarded life recognizes its own limits. Humility allows a person to receive correction. To seek Wisdom, and to remain teachable.

Pride weakens vigilance. Humility strengthens it.

Dependence on God. A guarded life does not rely solely on personal strength. It remains aware that Wisdom comes from God. Protection ultimately comes from God.

Discernment is sustained through relationship with Him. Dependence keeps guarding from becoming self-reliance.

Steadiness. Guarding is not dramatic; it is quiet consistency. It is a guarded life that does not overreact. It does not chase every disturbance. It remains anchored in truth. Steadiness prevents both panic and carelessness.

Guarding the spirit is not a moment of intensity but a way of living. When attention remains clear, obedience remains steady, and the heart remains aligned with God. The guard does not need to be forced. It remains naturally in place.

GOVERN YOURSELF ACCORDINGLY

As a Believer, you cannot be weak or ungoverned and then surprised by the results.

"Govern yourselves accordingly" is an old-school governance phrase. It means to assume responsibility for conduct. It means to act with foresight, and to order your behavior without external enforcement. Scripture assumes self-governance everywhere:

- "Keep your heart…"
- "Watch your life and doctrine…"
- "Let each examine himself…"
- "Rule your own house well…"

God does not micromanage maturity. He expects governance.

Self-governance matters in unguarded hours. Unguarded hours expose whether a person has awareness, order, internal restraint, practiced authority. If someone does not govern themselves while awake, they will not suddenly become governed when asleep.

This is why exhaustion reveals character and why hunger exposes priorities. Fatigue uncovers governance gaps. Esau, for example, did not lack inheritance. He lacked self-governance in the moment it mattered.

Governance is not optional. Self-governance is not optional. Scripture does not treat self-governance as a personality trait or spiritual gift. It treats it as a responsibility. To govern oneself is to assume stewardship over appetite, impulse, decision, and delegation—especially under strain. Esau did not lose his birthright because he was evil, but because he was unwilling to govern himself when hungry. Fatigue does not remove responsibility; it tests whether governance exists.

Many abdicate spiritual responsibility under the guise of humility, asking others to do what they themselves refuse to do. But delegation without oversight is not wisdom—it is avoidance. There is no guarantee that those who claim to be watching, praying, or standing in the gap are actually doing so. Scripture does not teach blind outsourcing of spiritual responsibility. It teaches order.

Self-governance does not mean doing everything alone. It means knowing what cannot be abandoned, even when help is present. It means refusing to trade inheritance for relief, or authority for comfort. In unguarded hours, governance is not suspended. It is either present—or absent.

The spirit man is not a substitute for self-governance. The spirit man is an instrument of self-governance. It's not that your spirit man has to do everything so you don't have to. But as Christians we must govern wisely by assigning what can be assigned, without abandoning what belongs to you.

Instruction to the spirit man" is legitimate; it flows from governance, not avoidance. Govern yourself. order what must be ordered. delegate wisely. rest without forfeiting inheritance.

In ancient Hebrew culture, a boy was not treated as a man simply because he grew older. He was recognized as a man when he was considered capable of self-governance, responsibility, covenant, accountability. Standing under the Law on his own; That is the age of authority.

Age 13, Bar Mitzvah (Son of the Commandment). At 13, a Jewish boy became Bar Mitzvah — literally, *"Son of the commandment."* This did not mean celebration of maturity, social coming-of-age, or permission to have fun. It meant that he is now personally responsible before God for his obedience to the Law.

Many believers are not weak; they are ungoverned. I reiterate: "Govern yourselves accordingly" — not Baptist, just biblical.

Because governance is work, too many want someone else to pray, someone else to hear God, someone else to stand watch someone else to "go up the mountain/"

And in doing so, they quietly abandon what was entrusted to *them*. That's not humility; that's abdication. Delegation without governance is abdication. Divine help does not replace responsibility; it partners with it. . Like my high school friend with the very nice sports car or other gifts that man or God has given you. That's not humility. It could be fear, ignorance, laziness—no matter the motivation, it's abdication.

Handling your spiritual business yourself prevents spiritual laziness, prevents celebrity-minister dependency, which can lead to idolatry. It prevents magical thinking. It honors both authority and restraint.

Do not abdicate your throne, little k, king; see to it yourself.

ABDICATION

" — the emphasis is your own. When it is something that you can do yourself, but you don't--, when that something requires authority that you are not stepping into and using, then that is abdication. Dereliction of duty and abdication of position and power—authority. And God breathed on him and made him a living being. You can breathe on your own, that's an authority, a power, an ability. No one wants a machine to do it for them if they can do it.

Scripture does not say hire someone to work it out for you, outsource it, assume it's handled because someone else is spiritual. It says, *"Work out your own salvation with fear and trembling.*

Not in panic, but in sobriety. The command assumes participation, effort, responsibility, personal engagement. Salvation is received freely. Formation is not passive.

You can't send someone else to the gym for you. You don't hire someone to shower on your behalf. You don't outsource breathing, eating, or sleeping. Some things cannot be delegated without becoming absurd.

Spiritual formation belongs in that category.

Scripture tells us to work out our own salvation—not to hire someone else to work it out for us. No one can go to the gym on your behalf and give you strength. No one can shower for you and keep you clean. Some responsibilities are personal by design. They cannot be outsourced without becoming meaningless. Spiritual governance is one of them.

There is a difference between receiving help and surrendering responsibility. Scripture never forbids counsel, intercession, or community—but it never replaces self-governance with them either. What belongs to you cannot be transferred simply because you are tired, busy, or human. Divine help partners with responsibility; it does not replace it.

> Examine yourselves, whether ye be in the faith; prove your own selves. (2 Corinthians 13:5)

Scripture does not say to examine others on your behalf. It does not say to outsource discernment or rely on borrowed assurance. It calls for honest self-assessment—especially when pressure, fatigue, or testing is present. Examination is a form of governance. It keeps inheritance from being traded away quietly.

Unguarded hours do not excuse abdication. They reveal whether governance exists. When the body is tired and the mind is dull, what has been practiced will surface. This is why self-governance matters long before exhaustion arrives. What you refuse to govern while alert will not suddenly become ordered when you sleep.

- Unguarded hours exist
- Fatigue and distraction lower defenses
- Self-governance is required
- Therefore, order must be established before rest

Some things cannot be delegated. Spiritual governance is one of them.

Unguarded hours do not excuse abdication. They reveal whether governance exists. When the body is tired and the mind is dull, what has been practiced will surface. This is why self-governance matters long before exhaustion arrives. What you refuse to govern while alert will not suddenly become ordered when you sleep.

WHAT IS THE INNER MAN?

Scripture consistently distinguishes between the outer man (the physical person, subject to fatigue and decay), and the inner man (the regenerated spirit, capable of discernment and strength beyond physical limits)

This distinction is not metaphorical. It is functional.

Paul writes of the "inner man" being renewed even while the outer man grows weary. Jesus distinguishes between a willing spirit and weak flesh. Proverbs states that "the spirit of man sustains him in times of sickness."

The inner man is not emotion, imagination, or self-talk. It is the regenerated human spirit—made alive by God, indwelt by the Holy Spirit, and capable of discernment, resistance, and obedience beyond physical stamina.

Mature believers recognize this intuitively. Beginners often feel it long before they have language for it. This book uses the term *spirit man* to describe this inner reality—not to mystify it, but to speak of it plainly.

The inner man does not replace God. He does not act independently of the Holy Spirit.

The spirit man (inner man) is not sovereign. He is governed, trained, and directed. And in unguarded hours, whether or not he has been strengthened and instructed matters greatly.

So, who do you lean on? Holy Spirit. God? Jesus? Angels? What instruments have been put in place for you? He will not forsake us, He will not leave us comfortless. He will not leave us powerless. He will not leave us twisting in the wind.

BUILD UP YOUR MOST HOLY FAITH

Building up your most holy faith. Building up your inner man. know what strengthens you, and know what weakens you — especially in siege.

What builds the spirit man?

These are not techniques. They are conditions under which the spirit of man remains strong, clear, and resilient. It is a strong spirit that ensures that a man does not have unguarded hours.

1. Proximity to God

- Drawing near without agenda
- Being with God without asking for outcomes
- Quiet presence rather than constant petition

The spirit is strengthened by **nearness**, not activity.

2. Truthful Stillness

- Silence that listens

- Stillness that waits
- Restraint that refuses to interfere

The spirit grows when it is not forced to perform.

3. Scripture as Alignment, Not Ammunition

- Reading to understand God's nature
- Letting Scripture correct posture
- Allowing the Word to govern timing

The spirit is nourished by **alignment**, not argument.

4. Obedience Without Immediate Reward

- Doing what is right when it doesn't "work"
- Waiting when obedience feels unproductive

This builds deep spiritual muscle.

5. Integrity of Thought

- Refusing to rehearse fear
- Not entertaining imagined outcomes
- Guarding what is allowed to live in the mind

The spirit strengthens when the mind is not feeding it noise.

6. Rest

- Actual rest, not distraction

- Letting the body be cared for
- Allowing limits

The spirit does not thrive in exhaustion.

But ye, beloved, building up yourselves on your most holy faith, praying in the Holy Ghost,

Keep yourselves in the love of God, looking for the mercy of our Lord Jesus Christ unto eternal life.

And of some have compassion, making a difference:

And others save with fear, pulling them out of the fire; hating even the garment spotted by the flesh.

Now unto him that is able to keep you from falling, and to present you faultless before the presence of his glory with exceeding joy, (Jude 20-24)

Foremost, prayer makes much power available for the one who is praying. The above verse tells us to pray in the Holy Ghost. I will not apologize for teaching what praying in the Spirit is.

It is:

- Your own personal prayer language given by the Holy Spirit of God. It is not unknown words, syllables, or phrases spoken at random in assorted settings, especially to 'show' people that you 'have the Holy Spirit.
- Speaking in tongues is an unknown language that is unknown to you, but know to whomever is hearing you speak. It is their native or understood

language and you are saying something to them that God wants them to hear.

- Speaking in tongues us when a person is unctioned by the Holy Spirit with an utterance, in public (usually) and THERE IS SOMEONE THERE TO INTERPRET WHAT WAS JUST SAID. I've heard people 'speak in tongues' and then interpret what they themselves just said. Hey, I'm not God, but couldn't they have just spoken in English or whatever language that the people there would understand?

So, you build up your most holy faith **PRAYING** in the Holy Ghost. Speaking in public or 'giving a word' is not **praying**; it is speaking or in some cases prophesying.

In the Book of Jude it says: **PRAYING.**

Now you know. Praise God.

Conversely, this is what breaks down or diminishes the spirit man. These things often look harmless — especially under pressure — but they erode strength quietly.

1. Constant Self-Rescue Attempts

- Repeatedly trying new angles
- Forcing movement when restrained
- Refusing to accept "wait"

This drains spiritual strength because it resists governance.

2. Fear-Based Decision Making

- Acting to relieve anxiety
- Making permanent choices under pressure
- Moving simply to feel control

Fear doesn't just affect emotions — it **weakens discernment**.

3. Over-Consumption of Noise

- Endless sermons, opinions, videos, commentary
- Looking for confirmation everywhere
- Needing external voices constantly

The spirit is diminished by **over-input**.

4. Transactional Spirituality

- Trying to give, pray, or act to force outcomes
- Bargaining with God
- Measuring obedience by results

This shifts trust into effort — and that weakens the inner man.

5. Resentment and Comparison

- Watching others' timelines too closely

- Measuring your season against someone else's
- Quiet bitterness about delay

Comparison fractures spiritual strength.

6. Neglect of the Body

- Sleep deprivation
- Ignoring physical limits
- Treating rest as unspiritual

The spirit is housed somewhere. Ignoring the vessel in which it is houses weakens both the person who houses it, the physical structure as well it jeopardizes the inhabitant.

In seasons of siege, the spirit must be protected. Certain postures strengthen it. Others quietly diminish it. Wisdom lies not in doing more, but in guarding what God is sustaining.

DONE-FOR-YOU MENTALITY

Salvation is finished. Formation is not. Formation of man, his conforming is not. Deliverance can be received. Governance must be learned. Grace is free. Maturity is costly.

This volume is about guarding in the night hours of the soul. It is about not being taken by the frailties that are common to man such as deception, distraction, and so on. It is about not abdicating responsibility and getting someone else to do the spiritual things for you. You're supposed to be growing spiritually; if you do not spiritual work, you will never grow spiritually. Growth is part of your conforming to the image of Christ.

A "done-for-you" mindset directly undermines all of that.

If someone believes "Jesus did it all, so I don't need to do anything else," then they will neglect watchfulness. They will confuse Grace with disengagement. They will resist discipline. That same person will reject responsibility. Eventually they will collapse under siege while at the same time still calling it faith.

Easy-street theology only survives when nothing is at stake. Under pressure, it fails. Every time, except for the Mercy of God.

- "That belief will not carry you."
- "Grace does not remove responsibility."
- "Inheritance still requires stewardship."

You can't be passive. Anti-passivity masquerading as belief will not work. Salvation is not a concierge service. God is not a spiritual delivery app. Faith is not spiritual automation.

- Establish what strengthens your spirit man.
- Avoid what weakens the spirit man.
- before or after self-governance is discussed

Salvation is not an exemption from responsibility; it is the beginning of it. Take responsibility, guard your life and those under your care and charge, else the unguarded hours are like doors and windows flung wide open. It is like a house without a roof so that anything flying over can just drop in. They aren't coming to visit; they are coming to steal, kill, and destroy.

LOW-KEY SAVED

Not getting saved won't let you off the hook.

Some people think they are saved because grandma is saved, like it's inherited. These people think they can be low-key saved because Grandma is saved. Being saved is not inherited.

Some think they can be saved and still be cool--, that is remain in the world. That's doublemindedness and it doesn't work either. Choose ye this day.

Yeah take your grandma to church. You may even have the same last name as your grandma, but none of that makes you saved. The pastor could know your name, but that doesn't make you saved.

You could know Scripture and be posting it online, but that doesn't make you saved. *Knowing church* doesn't make you saved. Church does not constitute a relationship with God.

If you are in a relationship but you never talk to the person and you have never committed to having a relationship with a person; then you have no relationship. So, you know where they live; you sit in their house but there is no communication, not connection; is no relationship. Knowing a person and that person knows you and committing to relationship, that's how the connection is created.

Not knowing church doesn't mean you are not saved, either. I had only gone to one church my entire childhood, but I didn't know how other people and other churches do church. Even if you don't *know church,* if you have accepted Jesus as your Lord and Savior for yourself, then you are saved.

Being saved is not all; now you begin to work out your salvation. There is work to do, but now you have the Grace and the empowerment to do it. Before salvation you had nothing. Not even hope.

Grandma's salvation won't get you into the Kingdom. A lot of people are saved and have accepted Jesus for themselves and may not know all the ways people hold church. They may not know all praise or worship songs. Some churches have dancers, Chrisitan rock, Christian rap, Christian jazz—and some still have hymn books. Even if you don't know the music and all the Scriptures, chapter and verse but if you are saved, then you are saved. Accepted the Lord Jesus into their hearts and made your confession of faith; then you are saved.

The goal is to live victoriously in Christ. After reading, studying, meditating and leaning on those verses as well as praying them those verses will become alive to you. The Word will keep you.

Unless the Lord watch, he that watches … in vain.

God can still be transcribed into words and still be alive. He will still be God. It will minister to you; get to know the life in the Word, the Spirit in the Word.

Chapter is the street your friend lives on and verse is the house number… that your friend lives on. Chapter and verse are not as important as the life in the Word. It is the life in the Word that is ministering to your life. Amen.

If you haven't been baptized in water but you've made your confession of faith then you are still saved. If you have not accepted Jesus as your Lord and Savior, then you have no one watching over you. Even if you are in church on a regular.

Grandma can't do for you what you should be doing for yourself after you are an adult, HOWEVER **the compound effect of multiple family members praying the SAME thing is glorious for individuals in the family, as well as for the whole bloodline.**

Those prayers stand guard at night, so the hours are not unguarded.

So are you saved or not? Is anyone? We can't judge what is in their heart, but the Bible says that we will know them by their fruit. If you are low-key saved, then you will have low-key fruit. Little fruit, no fruit, plastic fruit, rotten fruit.

Knowing Scriptures doesn't make you saved. The devil knows the Scriptures. The devil never sleeps, and has been around for thousands of years and is always looking for a loophole in the Bible so he can accuse that man to God. He may know the Bible better than a lot of Christians.

You have to adult in your salvation. See to it yourself.

Grandma's prayers matter. Grandma's faith blesses the family. Grandma's obedience creates covering. But Grandma cannot repent for you, obey for you, watch for you, govern your mind, steward your adulthood. A person is not saved because Grandma is saved.

A person is not saved just because they watch Christian channels. You're not saved just because Grandma prays for you. You have to accept Jesus for yourself.

Family members praying the same thing in unity, over time, with shared language, with shared posture creates reinforcement, continuity, memory, and endurance. That's not Grandma saving anyone. That's a bloodline learning to agree with God.

Low key saved is not really saved at all. Just asking God for things and stuff is not saved. Renew your relationship with God so you are not deceived or disappointed.

ORDERING THE INNER MAN BEFORE SLEEP

Ordering the inner man before rest. God promises to give sleep to His beloved, but what follows is not a prayer to God. It is not petition. It is not pleading. It is not fear-driven. And it is not meant to replace prayer, Scripture, discipline, or discernment.

What follows is instruction given to the regenerated inner man—spoken deliberately at a moment when the body must rest and conscious vigilance can no longer be maintained.

God does not sleep. But man does; the human body does. Scripture makes clear that while the outer man is subject to fatigue, the inner man can be strengthened, governed, and ordered.

There are seasons when vigilance has been prolonged beyond what is sustainable. Not because of disobedience. Not because of sin. But because of responsibility, warfare, caregiving, leadership, pressure, or extended strain.

There are hours when attention is depleted. Discernment is dulled by fatigue. The environment feels unsafe, unstable, or unpredictable. Rest feels risky, yet exhaustion makes wakefulness impossible. These are unguarded hours.

The danger of unguarded hours is not that a person sleeps, the danger is that nothing has been ordered to stand watch when they do.

Sleep is not the enemy. This is not about avoiding sleep. Scripture explicitly says that God gives sleep to His beloved. Rest is not negligence. Fatigue is not failure.

The issue is not *whether* the body rests. The issue is that nothing should be left unattended when it does.

The spiritual realm does not pause because the physical realm disengages. That is not a threat—it is simply reality. Wisdom does not deny reality. Wisdom orders itself accordingly.

Authority, not anxiety. What follows must not be read as fear of the night, dreams, or unseen activity. Fear leads to hypervigilance which leads to exhaustion, which leads to collapse.

This practice does the opposite.

It acknowledges human limits without surrendering authority. It does not attempt to control everything. It assigns what can be assigned and rests where rest is required.

This is not obsession with the enemy. It is refusal to leave anything ungoverned.

This section is not written for beginners, though beginners may encounter it. It is written for those who have already prayed and prayed. You have already fasted. You have already stood watch. You have already exercised discernment, and now you are simply tired.

It is for the faithful who discovered that endurance, not enthusiasm, was required.

If you are not in such a season, you do not need to adopt this practice. If you are, you will recognize it immediately.

Scripture distinguishes between the outer man, which grows weary. and the inner man, which can be strengthened. This distinction is not symbolic. It is functional.

Just as leaders assign watches, parents give instructions before leaving, and commanders issue orders before nightfall, so too the inner man can be spoken to, aligned, and directed. This is not independence from God. It is submission to the order God already established.

The Holy Spirit remains sovereign. Authority remains delegated, not assumed. Correction remains welcomed. Nothing here bypasses God. Everything here relies on Him.

HOW TO READ WHAT FOLLOWS

A Transcript of Instruction Given Under Exhaustion

What follows is presented **as it was given**. It has not been polished into something gentle. It has not been reduced to a formula. It has not been softened for mass consumption. It is a transcript of instruction given under exhaustion.

Read it. Slowly. Soberly, without attempting to imitate what does not apply to you. This is not a ritual. It is not a nightly requirement. It is a response to a specific kind of season.

One governing truth**.** Before you read the instruction itself, understand this: God does not require consciousness to maintain coverage. But He does require order. What follows is order. *(The instruction text follows here, unchanged.)*

This text is not for beginners. And that is okay. It is for seasoned Believers, leaders, intercessors, caregivers, and people who have stayed alert longer than they should have had to

IN WARFARE SO LONG

Have you ever been in warfare, in battle so long that you are just plain tired? Exhausted. You have been fasting, praying, praying, fasting. You don't want to close your eyes because if you do something weird is trying to come at you. And if you go to sleep your dreams, or whatever happens in your dreams seems unbearable, it's too much.

But you are exhausted. You can't even think straight. You don't even look right. And you think, if you could rest a little you could regroup and think of what to do next. But you don't want to go to sleep because you don't trust your environment. You don't trust what's going on around you or what you think or fear will go on if you are not awake, alert, sitting upright – lights on, looking around. Or praying—like all night.

God gives sleep to His beloved. And you know you are beloved of God.

Should you sleep? Even for a minute. Dream afflictions. You're so tired. You're tired of being awake and you're tired of what happens in the dream.

Or maybe you're just tired because you are looking out for, looking after, tending to, taking care of everything by yourself or taking care of everyone else and yes, they really do need you, whether they say thank you, or not. Maybe they don't have anyone else – it's all on you.

BUT YOU ARE SO TIRED.

I've been there.

AND THIS IS WHAT THE LORD DID FOR ME WHEN I WAS THERE. THIS IS WHAT THE HOLY SPIRIT TAUGHT ME AND HE TOLD ME TO SHARE IT WITH YOU.

You've prayed all you know to pray. Binding, *loosing*, warfare, fasting. You've commanded the night, you're ready to wake up in the morning and command the morning and the day. Deal with the dreams of the previous night. Repented, asked for Mercy. Everything.

One night, not that long ago, when I just couldn't take it anymore—at the point of exhaustion, I decided (by help of the Holy Spirit) to have a talk with my spirit man. This is not a prayer; it is a directive to my spirit man.

TO MY SPIRIT MAN

My Spirit Man, I'm Going to Sleep Right Now; I'm Tired. *You Got This?* Yes. You Got This.

My Spirit Man, I'm about to go to sleep right now. I'm tired. I will get good rest tonight. Your assignment, spirit man is to take care of things while I am asleep. Take care of everything. You are able, you are prepared, you have the Word of God in you. So, as I sleep you stick right beside the Holy Spirit. Do not let him out of your sight and you do not leave His side. Wherever he goes, you go. Whatever He tells you to do, you do that.

You do not go anywhere the Holy Spirit doesn't go. You do not go anywhere without the Holy Spirit.

You will respond to no evil calls.

You will respond to no evil summons.

You will respond to no evil instructions.

You will go to no coven. No graveyard. No satanic circle. No evil council meeting if called or summoned there. You do not spend time with witches, warlocks, wizards, occultist or the like.

You will not walk in the counsel of the wicked.

You will not stand in the midst of sinners,

Nor sit in the seat of the scornful,

Nor will you sit in the congregation of the wicked.

I have hated the congregation of evil doers, and I will not sit with the wicked, Psalm 26:5. NEITHER WILL YOU.

You will take care of things while I am asleep. You will not let anything happen to me while I am asleep. Nothing bad will happen to my spirit, soul, or body because you got this, right?

If you hear any evil thing regarding me, you will cast down that evil imagination immediately.

If you hear evil incantations, hexes, vexes, jinxes, evil plans, evil council meetings, denounce those words, cancel them, break their power, dismantle them, condemn the language they speak, the words they speak, and the speaker. You know warfare, so break those evil assignments if and when you hear them.

My spirit man, you will be progressive—anything that tries to call you back to soul ties, sin, Egypt, or into iniquity, bondage or yokes, you resist that.

Any trap, ditch, pit or other entrapment set for you or me, you will not fall for it, you will not fall into it, and you will escape like a bird from every snare, in the Name of Jesus.

I will be resting soundly, so when I awake I will be well-rested. As the Holy Spirit of God ministers to me in any way such as healing teaching, impartations, activations of the Spirit, in the Name of Jesus.

If the Holy Spirit tells or teaches you anything in the night be sure to remember it and be sure I know about it when I wake up and that I understand it, in the Name of Jesus.

If the Holy Spirit casts a vision be sure we are empowered and we know what to do to run with that, in the Name of Jesus.

If the Holy Spirit gives you an inspired idea, be sure to retain it. Ask for clarity if necessary so we will know exactly what to do.

If the Holy Spirit shows you blessings, abundance, wealth, houses or anything that belongs to my Peace, be sure to accept it. If it is locked away, ask Him and the Holy Spirit to bind and take away the strongman from the gate or door.

When the door to all those blessings is opened to you, be sure you speak to the door that it remains open for you, forever, even into your generations. Take what you should take in that moment, and ask exactly what it is for, how it is to be used, and how to bring it to the Earth realm. Perhaps you can ask the Holy Spirit to send it or send it by Angels of Blessings or Angels of Wealth.

My spirit man, if you see, find out about or sense that any part of my humanity is in captivity or bondage, ask the Holy Spirit for deliverance from that bondage and ask the Angels or the LORD to bring any and all of my parts out of captivity. The Holy Spirit is the Spirit of Deliverance.

If the Holy Spirit solves a problem in my life, be sure to retain that and share it with me when I am awake.

If the Holy Spirit sends correction, we receive that in the Name of Jesus. We listen, we hear, we obey: we do not grieve or quench the Holy Spirit, ever.

So, if anything evil tries to approach me while I am asleep, handle that. The mighty Angels of God have watch over me, so they are here; call on them if necessary.

Use the shield of faith to block any evil arrow that may be sent at me, and also the Word of God which you are well versed in.

Spirit man: YOU DO NOT EAT ANY EVIL or UNGODLY THING. YOU DO NOT DRINK ANYTHING. DO NOT LET ANY THING OR ANY ONE UNGODLY TOUCH YOU OR ME. I WILL BE RESTING, AND HEALING, AND BEING MADE WHOLE.

IF WE ARE FORTUNATE TO GO TO THE THRONE OF GOD BE SURE WE ARE ABIDING BY ALL PROTOCOLS, HE IS THE KING OF KINGS, AND BE SURE WE ARE WORSHIPPING AND WORSHIPFUL.

IF ANY SICKNESS, DISORDER OR DISEASE TRIES TO COME UPON ME, SEND IT BACK, REJECT IT, IN THE NAME OF JESUS.

IF THERE IS SOME TYPE OF ILLNESS GOING ON IN MY BODY THAT I AM UNAWARE OF, THE HOLY SPIRIT CAN HEAL ME. UNTIL THAT HEALING YOU ARE MY SPIRIT MAN – THE SPIRIT OF MAN SUSTAINS HIM IN TIMES OF SICKNESS.

IF ANY TROUBLE TRIES TO COME UPON ME, BEAR ME UP UNTIL THAT TROUBLE GOES, THE SPIRIT OF MAN SUSTAINS HIM IN TIMES OF TROUBLE.

Sustain me.

IF THERE IS ANY UNGODLY DARKNESS, YOU ARE THE CANDLE; YOU ARE THE CANDLE OF THE LORD. The spirit of man is the candle of the LORD.

My spirit man: you've got this. I will rest. I will both lay me down in safety and I will sleep, because the LORD gives me rest. My spirit man doesn't sleep; he's watching and the Holy Spirit is here because the LORD watches because we do not watch in vain, in the Name of Jesus.

I will both lay me down in safety and I will rest – the LORD gives sleep to His beloved; I am beloved of the Lord and the Angels of the LORD also are encamped around about me because I hold the Lord in awe and admiration. The fear of the LORD is the beginning of Wisdom, knowledge, and understanding.

The Angels of the Lord are encamped, they keep me in all my ways so that I do not worry about enemies, darkness, pestilence, or danger – it will not come near me, in the Name of Jesus.

Spirit man, in the spirit the LORD has prepared daily benefits and tender mercies – be sure you collect those things from the LORD we will be needing them for the day tomorrow.

Scatter all parasites, evil birds, emptiers, wasters, scatterers, devourers and destroyers, keep them away from today's blessings, in the Name of Jesus.

My spirit man, you are strong, wise and very courageous; you can handle this and so much more. Stay in the Light and stay in step with the Holy Spirit, and I will rest now, in the Name of Jesus. Thank you, GOD BLESS YOU.

AFTER THE NIGHT IS ORDERED

When the inner man has been instructed and the body is permitted to rest, something shifts. The night no longer feels like abandonment. Sleep no longer feels like surrender. Dreams no longer feel like an ungoverned space.

Rest becomes restorative instead of fragile. People wake differently—not necessarily energized, but re-centered.

Discernment sharpens. Clarity returns. Fear quiets. Not because nothing happened in the night—but because what *could* happen was not left unattended. Daylight discernment improves. Ordering the inner man does not only affect sleep. It affects boundaries, reactions, sensitivity to warning, resistance to old patterns, recognition of subtle compromise. People find themselves less reactive, less easily drawn, less confused by emotional residue. The watch that stood at night leaves a trace of order in the day.

Rest without guilt. Perhaps the greatest change is that people stop apologizing for being human. Sleep is no longer viewed as weakness. Rest is no longer feared.

Limits are acknowledged without shame. The inner man has been trained. The outer man is allowed to recover. This is not passivity. It is stewardship.

A quiet kind of authority emerges, not bravado or intensity. It is something quieter. There is confidence without strain. Authority without volume. Peace without denial. The night does not need to be conquered; it needs to be ordered. When it is, the beloved sleep of God's people becomes what it was always meant to be: rest, not risk.

My Spirit Man is executive spiritual governance under duress. It belongs to the same category as David "commanding his soul. " And, it is in the same category as Jesus saying, "The spirit indeed is willing, but the flesh is weak." It goes along with Paul distinguishing *outer man* and *inner man.*

It goes with watch assignments in Scripture; we are to set a watch, a prayer watch not a timepiece on your arm.

This prayer is wartime delegation when the commander must sleep. That distinction is critical—and once named, this text becomes *legitimate*, not strange.

My Spirit Man gives permission to rest without surrender. It validates exhaustion without calling it failure It names a fear many people are ashamed to admit, "I'm too tired to stay alert, but I don't trust the night."

ANGELS WATCHING OVER ME

Scripture does not teach automatic, thoughtless spiritual coverage. The Bible never teaches things like, "You're asleep, therefore angels are watching no matter what." That would remove responsibility, order, and discernment. Our parents may teach that to us as little children, but it's not in the Bible.

Angelic ministry in Scripture is **assigned**, **<u>commanded by God</u>**, responsive to His will, and often connected to alignment—not mere unconsciousness.

Sleep alone is not a switch that activates protection of any kind. Did you pray about it? Did you ask God? Did you look up and find the Scriptures that support it?

Scripture *does* teach watchfulness that does not depend on human wakefulness. So when you go to sleep, then what? That is what this book has been about.

What Scripture *does* teach is more precise—and more reassuring: "He who keeps Israel neither slumbers nor sleeps." So, yes, God is 'keeping' us--, 'keeping Israel." Are we in that ilk?

The angel of the LORD encamps around those who fear Him. (Psalm 34:7)

Unless the LORD watches the city, the watchman stays awake in vain. (Psalm 127:1)

That verse, the Bible does not say *you* must stay awake. It does not say Angels work automatically. It says the Lord watches.

Angels are ministers of *His* watching—not replacements for it.

The real question is not "Are angels watching?" It is: *What has been ordered?*

Sleep creates absence of conscious governance. Scripture consistently addresses absence not with anxiety, but with **order**. Set a watch. Assign guards. Give instruction before nightfall. Commit what you cannot carry to the Lord, and Amen.

You are not assuming Angelic coverage. You are aligning with Divine order before rest. That's the difference between presumption and stewardship.

Angels respond to God's Will—not human panic. Angels are not summoned by human fear, insomnia, or repetition. They respond to God's command, God's covenant, God's purposes.

In My Spirit Man, it says to my spirit, "Remain aligned with the Holy Spirit. Respond to no summons outside Him. Call on what God has already appointed."

Amen again.

Can a Believer rest in angelic protection while asleep?

Yes—but not because they are asleep.

They rest because the Lord watches. Order has been established. Responsibility has not been abandoned. Vigilance has been delegated, not dropped. That is why Scripture can say, "I will both lie down and sleep in peace…" Not because nothing could happen—but because nothing is unattended.

Angels obey God and the Voice of the Word of God; they don't just automatically to what you want or need. Before sleep, order what must be ordered and established so that what must remain attentive will remain. That honors God's Sovereignty. That acknowledges human limitation, Angelic assignment, and spiritual reality.

Sleep, even when you desperately need sleep, does not itself guarantee coverage. The Lord does. Angels do not replace vigilance; they minister according to Divine order. Rest is not trust unless responsibility has first been rightly placed.

So, no—we do not assume Angelic watch because we are asleep. But yes—we may rest because the Lord watches, and because what must remain alert has not been left ungoverned. That is not superstition; that is Wisdom.

Angels *do* respond to assignment — but not autonomous human assignment. Scripture is clear that Angels are **sent**, commissioned, assigned, stationed, dispatched. They are not random responders.

Are they not all ministering spirits, **sent** to serve those who will inherit salvation?"
(Hebrews 1:14)

Angels respond to assignments that originate in God's Will and order, not from human will detached from God.

We do not worship Angels. The first record of an angel who wanted to act independent of God was kicked out of Heaven. That same angel is the one who said he would exalt his own throne. Why would he want a throne? For worship. We do not worship angels, and that's the clearest reason why right there.

Assignment does not mean command *over* angels, when we are operating in alignment with God's Divine order that already includes Angelic ministry

In Scripture, God assigns Angels. Angels obey **<u>God</u>**. Humans *align with* God's assignments, not the other way around. That alignment can include prayer, obedience, agreement, stewardship, and sometimes delegation of responsibility under God

JESUS was all God could have called 12 legions of Angels. Jesus, who was all man did not call Angels. Do we see the picture here?

God does give His Angels charge over us, but Angels are consistently associated with gates, thresholds, watches, transitions, protection of Covenant purpose, and movement between realms. We are not all-God and we cannot deploy legions of Angels in the same way that Jesus could have but acted with spiritual restraint.

And notice this: Angels often appear **after order is established**, not before.

- *After* Lot is instructed
- *After* Daniel prays
- *After* Peter is sleeping *between guards*
- *After* Jesus resists temptation
- *After* Elijah collapses — and is fed

Angelic activity follows Divine order — not chaos, not frenzy.

"I order myself under God, align with the Holy Spirit, refuse illegitimate summons, and rest, in the Name of Jesus. Amen."

We do not assign Angels on our own. We do not overreach as humans. We do acknowledge Divine hierarchy, and by setting right order, we create conditions where angelic assignment already in place is not resisted.

We do not pray to Angels; we do not invoke Angels. We do not interfere with the assignments of Angels.

Angels are not magical creatures that do everything we want or need like a robot or a fairy. They are not activated by sleep, nor summoned by fear. They respond to Divine assignment. When order is established and responsibility is rightly placed, what God has already assigned is not hindered. Angelic ministry is not assumed; it is aligned with. Order does not create protection — it cooperates with what God has already set in place.

Thia keeps authority intact, hierarchy intact, mystery intact, responsibility intact.

Angels do respond to assignment — but the assignment belongs to God. Our role is to order ourselves so that what He has already assigned is not resisted, contradicted, or left unattended.

Dear Reader: know that you shouldn't just assume that everything is fine but take correct and purposeful steps to be sure things are fine. Things (and Angels) don't just show up because you want them to.

Safety cannot just be assumed, else one could fall into unguarded hours where the enemy who is already crouched at the door is awaiting access. Even if you are totally exhausted from warfare be sure to set order for the night hours. Just as sure as you'd lock your door, shut your windows and set your alarm, set spiritual order before you rest.

Do not confuse rest with abdication. Do not confuse belief with governance. Desire $\neq$ assignment. Do not rely on someone else to do it. Do not ignore spiritual warnings or inklings no matter if it is your BFF telling you, Don't worry, everything is fine. Maybe it is fine for them, for their life, for their family and business, but maybe it's different for you which is why you are getting the warning.

Discern every spirit. Establish right order as the watchman over things you are called to. Leave nothing unguarded or unattended.

Angelic ministry does not respond to desire, fatigue, or fear. It responds to Divine assignment.

ORDER PRECEDES REST

It would be a mistake to assume that everything is fine simply because one has decided to rest. Rest is not the same as order. Neither God nor His messengers are summoned by preference, need, or wishful thinking. Angelic ministry responds to divine assignment, not human desire. What is left unattended does not become safe because it is ignored. Wisdom takes deliberate, purposeful steps to ensure that what must remain governed is, before consciousness gives way to sleep.

Mature readers recognize Yes. Order precedes rest. “Yes. Assignment is real.” “Yes. Responsibility doesn’t disappear at night.” Both feel respected.

Peace does not come from assuming nothing will happen. It comes from knowing that nothing has been left unattended.

Unguarded Hours is a book for adults in the faith. Don't sell your birthright just because you're hungry like Esau. Don't just fall asleep 'hoping' just because you’re exhausted; don't give up just because you're human and so tired. You have divine resources; your spirit man is one of those divine resources with access to more Divine Help.

The Esau connection is exact—and important. Esau was not wicked in that moment. He was hungry, tired, and impulsive. He did not lose his birthright because he hated it. He lost it because he valued immediate relief over long-term authority.

Do not trade spiritual authority for temporary relief just because you are exhausted.

That is stewardship. We are called to stewardship and to wise stewardship. We are to possess our vessel with sanctification and honor…

There are principles for stewarded rest. Jesus said to the Disciples in the Garede of Gethsemane: "Can you watch and pray ONE hour?" In other words, Don't sleep when you should be praying or doing some other discipline of the faith. Don't sleep until you have completed your assignment.

Work while it is day because the night comes when no man can work.

GUARDING VS. HYPERVIGILANCE

Hypervigilance is not guarding—it's fear wearing the costume of Wisdom. Guarding is calm, steady awareness. Hypervigilance is constant tension. A guarded life is watchful but at Peace. A hypervigilant life is restless and suspicious. One protects the spirit. The other exhausts it.

How to Guard Without Becoming Hypervigilant

1. Stay Anchored in Peace

Guarding should not produce anxiety.

If watchfulness creates:

- constant dread
- suspicion of everyone
- inability to rest

then vigilance has crossed into fear.

A guarded life still allows the soul to remain at Peace with God.

2. Refuse to Interpret Everything as Threat

Hypervigilance turns every situation into danger.

Guarding recognizes that:

- most people are ordinary
- most events are neutral
- not every tension is an attack

Wisdom evaluates; fear assumes.

3. Maintain Rest

A person who never rests cannot remain discerning.

Guarding includes:

- sleep
- stepping away from conflict
- periods where nothing is analyzed

Rest protects discernment from becoming paranoia.

4. Stay Rooted in Truth, Not Suspicion

Hypervigilance lives on imagined scenarios.

Guarding responds only to real information.

It asks:

- What do I actually know?
- What is speculation?

Truth stabilizes vigilance.

5. Keep Healthy Relationships

Hypervigilance isolates people.

Guarded living still includes:

- trusted friendships
- wise counsel
- community

Isolation feeds suspicion.

Connection keeps discernment **balanced**.

5. Let God Carry What You Cannot Control. Hypervigilance tries to monitor everything.

Guarding recognizes that ultimate protection belongs to God.

A person does their part:

- watchfulness
- obedience
- discipline

Then they rest in God's sovereignty.

Guarding the spirit does not require constant tension. True vigilance is steady and peaceful. It pays attention without living in fear, and it rests in God even while remaining aware.

Watchfulness allows Peace.

The Guarded Person vs. The Hypervigilant Person

A guarded person is attentive but calm. They notice what matters, respond when necessary, and rest when nothing requires action. Their awareness is steady because it is rooted in truth and trust in God.

A hypervigilant person, by contrast, is constantly scanning for danger. Every situation feels like a potential threat, every interaction requires analysis, and rest becomes difficult because the mind never fully settles.

The guarded person lives with **clarity**. The hypervigilant person lives with **tension**.

One protects the spirit through Wisdom, the other exhausts it through fear.

True watchfulness allows a person to remain peaceful while still paying attention. It does not require constant suspicion.

GUARD THE QUIET HOURS

Every life has unguarded hours. Moments when attention fades. Moments when fatigue sets in. Moments when nothing seems urgent and everything feels safe. It is in those moments that decisions are made quietly. Permissions are granted subtly. And the direction of a life begins to shift.

Most people do not lose their way in a single, dramatic moment. They lose it gradually—in hours that seemed ordinary at the time.

The call of Scripture has never been to fear. It has always been to **watch**. Not with anxiety. Not with suspicion. But with clarity. With awareness. With responsibility.

God is Sovereign.

The Earth has been entrusted to mankind. And within that trust, each person has been given something to guard. A life. A calling. A soul. A set of gates. No one else can fully guard these for you.

Not family. Not leaders. Not friends. Others may help. Others may warn. Others may stand watch alongside you. But the responsibility remains personal.

The watchman does not stand his post because danger is certain; he stands because danger is possible, and because what he guards is valuable. Perhaps even priceless.

There will be hours when you are tired. Hours when you would rather not think. Hours when it would be easier to assume everything is fine. Those are the hours that matter. Not because something always happens. But because something **can**.

A guarded life is not built in moments of crisis. It is built in quiet moments of attention. Small decisions. Simple refusals. Steady awareness.

So guard the gates. Guard what you allow in. Guard what you agree with. Guard what you tolerate.

And when the hour grows quiet and the world grows still— remain watchful.

Because a life is rarely lost in public battle. Too many times, it is lost quietly… in unguarded hours. But Jesus does not want that even one would be lost.

MAN IS USEFUL....AND NEEDED.

Dear Reader:

Thank you for acquiring and reading this book. I pray that it has

Be strong in the Lord, and be blessed, in the Name of Jesus, Amen.

Dr. Marlene Miles

PS: If this book helped you, you are welcome to leave a short review on Amazon. Reviews help other readers discover the book.

If you enjoyed this book, here are some new releases by this author.

Christ of God (*The*) 3-book series

Christ of God, (*The*) Box Set, includes all three books

Other books on authority:

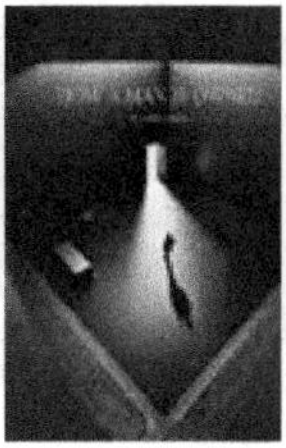

Prayerbooks by this author

There are some books that are only prayers. You just open up the book and pray.

Prayers Against Barrenness: *For Success in Business and Life*

Fruit of the Womb: *Prayers Against Barrenness*

Beauty Curses, *Warfare Prayers Against*
https://a.co/d/5Xlc20M

Courts of Marriage: Prayers for Marriage in the Courts of Heaven *(prayerbook)* https://a.co/d/cNAdgAq

Courtroom Warfare @ Midnight *(prayerbook)*
https://a.co/d/5fc7Qdp

Demonic Cobwebs *(prayerbook)* https://a.co/d/fp9Oa2H

Every Evil Bird https://a.co/d/hF1kh1O

Gates of Thanksgiving

Spirits of Death, Hell & the Grave, Pass Over Me and My House

Throne of Grace: Courtroom Prayer

Warfare Prayer Against Poverty
https://a.co/d/bZ61lYu

Prayer Manuals

FAKE FRIENDS: *Prayers Against Betrayers*

HOLIDAY WARFARE Prayer Manual (humorous) Surviving Family Gatherings All Year Long (without catching a case)

SOUL TIE Prayer Manual (The) Part of a 3-part series including a workbook.

MAD at DADDY Prayer Manual – part of a 3-part series including a workbook.

Healing the Sibling & Relative Wound Prayer Manual

Healing the Father-Son Wound Prayer Manual

Prayers Against Barrenness: *For Success in Business and Life*

Breaking Curses of the Mother Prayer Manual

Other books by this author

Abundance of Jesus (The) https://a.co/d/5gHJVed

AK: The Adventures of the Agape Kid

Already Married in the Spirit: *Why You May Not Be Married in the Natural*

AMONG SOME THIEVES https://a.co/d/dkYT4ZV

Ancestral Powers

Anti-Marriage, *The Spirit of*

Backstabbers https://a.co/d/gi8iBxf

Barrenness, *Prayers Against* https://a.co/d/feUltIs

Battlefield of Marriage, *The*

Beware of the Dog: Prayers Against Dogs in the Dream.

Bless Your Food: *Let the Dining Table be Undefiled* *https://a.co/d/6oPMRDv*

Blindsided: *Has the Old Man Bewitched You?* https://a.co/d/5O2fLLR

Break Free from Collective Captivity

Broken Spirits & Dry Bones

By Means of a Whorish Father

Caged Life: Get Out Alive! https://a.co/d/bwPbksX

Casting Down Imaginations

Christ of God (*The*) 3-book series

Christ of God, (*The*) Box Set, includes all three books

Churchzilla, The Wanna-Be, Supposed-to-be Bride of Christ https://a.co/d/eAf5j3x

Collateral Damage: *When What Happened Spiritually Was Your Fault*

Demonic Cobwebs (prayerbook)

Demonic Time Bombs

Demons Hate Questions

Devil Loves Trauma, *The*

Devil Weapons: Unforgiveness, Bitterness,…

The Devourers: Thieves of Darkness 2

Do Not Swear by the Moon

Don't Refuse Me, Lord (4 book series)

https://a.co/d/idP34LG

Dream Defilement

The Emptiers: *Thieves of Darkness, 1*
https://a.co/d/5I4n5mc

Entanglements: Illegal Knots Limiting Your Life

Evil Touch

Failed Assignment

Fantasy Spirit Spouse https://a.co/d/hW7oYbX

FAT Demons (The): *Breaking Demonic Curses*
https://a.co/d/4kP8wV1

The Fold (5-book series)

- The Fold (Book 1)
- Name Your Seed (Book 2)
- The Poor Attitudes of Money (3)
- Do Not Orphan Your Seed (4)
- For the Sake of the Gospel (5)
- My Sowing Journal

Gang Ups: Touch Not God's Anointed

Gathered: No Longer Scattered
https://a.co/d/1i5DPlX

Getting Rid of Evil Spiritual Food

https://a.co/d/i2L3WYQ

got HEALING? Verses for Life

got LOVE? Verses for Life https://a.co/d/8seXHPd

got HOPE? Verses for Life

got money? https://a.co/d/g2av41N

Has My Soul Been Sold? https://a.co/d/dyB8hhA

Here Come the Horns: *Skilled to Destroy* https://a.co/d/cZiNnkP

Hidden Sins: Hidden Iniquity

https://a.co/d/4Mth0wa

How to Dental Assist

How to Dental Assist2: Be Productive, Not Wasteful

How To Stay Prayed Up

How to STOP Being a Blind Witch or Warlock

I Take It Back

In Multiplying I Will Multiply Thee

Into Freedom:

Irresistible: Jesus' Triumphal Entry
https://a.co/d/d09IfEC

KNOW YOUR BATTLE: Stop Swinging Blindly — and Win Against Opponents, Adversaries & Enemies (Workbook) https://a.co/d/eOwFKlV

Legacy

Let Me Have A Dollar's Worth
https://a.co/d/h8F8XgE

Level the Playing Field

Living for the NOW of God
https://a.co/d/6bK5duE

Lose My Location https://a.co/d/crD6mV9

Love Breaks Your Heart

Mad At Daddy: Healing Father-Wounds that Affect Motherhood (book, workbook & prayer manual)

Made Perfect In Love

Mammon https://a.co/d/29yhMG7

Man Safari, *The*

Marriage Ed.: *Rules of Engagement & Marriage*

Made Perfect in Love

Money Hunters: Beware of Those

Money on the Altar https://a.co/d/4EqJ2Nr

Mulberry Tree, *The* https://a.co/d/9nR9rRb

Motherboard (The)- *Soul Prosperity Series*

Name Your Seed

Occupy: *Until I Return* https://a.co/d/bZ7ztUy

One Defining Day*: A Day When Dreams Come True*

Opponent, Adversary, or Enemy?: Fight The Right Battle with the Right Weapons

https://a.co/d/byQqEE2 & companion workbook: Know Your Battle

Plantation Souls

Players Gonna Play

Portals: Shut the Front Door: Prayers to Close Evil Portals.

Power Money: Nine Times the Tithe

https://a.co/d/gRt41gy

The Power to Get Wealth https://a.co/d/e4ub4Ov

Powers Above

The Robe, Part 1, The Lessons of Joseph

The Robe, Part II, The Lessons of Joseph

Seasons of Grief

Seasons of Siege: God Is Coming

Seasons of Waiting

Seasons of War

Second Marriage, Third--, *Any Marriage*

https://a.co/d/6m6GN4N

Seducing Spirits: Idolatry & Whoredoms

https://a.co/d/4Jq4WEs

Shut the Front Door: *Prayers to Close Portals*
https://a.co/d/cH4TWJj

Siege: *God Is Coming*

Sift You Like Wheat

Six Men Short: What Has Happened to all the Men?

SLAVE

Sleep Afflictions & Really Bad Dreams
https://a.co/d/f8sDmgv

Soul Prosperity soul prosperity series 3

https://a.co/d/5p8YvCN

Soul Ties: How Soul Ties Form, and How To Break Them (book, workbook & prayer manual)

Souls In Captivity

The Spirit of Anti-Marriage

The Spirit of Poverty https://a.co/d/abV2o2e

Spiritual Thieves https://a.co/d/eqPPz33

StarStruck- Triangular Power series.

SUNBLOCK- Triangular Power series.

The Swallowers: *Thieves of Darkness*, 3

Take It Back

This Is NOT That: How to Keep Demons from Coming at You

Time Is of the Essence

Too Many Wives: *Why You Have Lady Problems*

Tormenting Spirits https://a.co/d/dAogEJf

Toxic Souls

Triangular Power *(series)*, Powers Above, SUNBLOCK, Do Not Swear by the Moon, STARSTRUCK

TRIBE: *What Covenants Are Governing You…?*

Unbreak My Heart: *Don't Let Me Die*

Uncontested Doom

Ungovered Hunger: How Unchecked Appetite Dismantles Authority

Unguarded Hours, *The*

Unseen Life, *The* (forthcoming)

Upgrade: How to Get Out of Survival Mode Toxic Souls (Book 2 of series) , Legacy (Book 3 of series)

The Wasters: *Thieves of Darkness,* Bk 2
https://a.co/d/bUvI9Jo

What Have You to Declare? What Do You Have With You from Where You've Been?

When I Was A Child, *I Prayed As a Child*

When the Devourer is Rebuked
https://a.co/d/1HVv8oq

When The Table Is Set Against You

WTH? Get Me Out of This Hell
https://a.co/d/a7WBGJh

The Wilderness Romance ***(series)*** This series is about conducting a Godly relationship and marriage with

someone who is a Wilderness person. ***The Social Wilderness***

- ***The Sexual Wilderness***
- ***The Spiritual Wilderness***

Other Series

The Fold (a series on Godly finances) https://a.co/d/4hz3unj

Soul Prosperity Series https://a.co/d/bz2M42q

Spirit Spouse books

https://a.co/d/9VehDSo

https://a.co/d/97sKOwm

Battlefield of Marriage, The

https://a.co/d/eUDzizO

Players Gonna Play

https://a.co/d/2hzGw3N

Sent Spirit Spouse (can someone send you a spirit spouse? This book is not yet released.)

Matters of the Heart, Made Perfect in Love

https://a.co/d/70MQW3O , Love Breaks Your Heart https://a.co/d/4KvuQLZ, Unbreak My Heart https://a.co/d/84ceZ6M Broken Spirits & Dry Bones https://a.co/d/e6iedNP

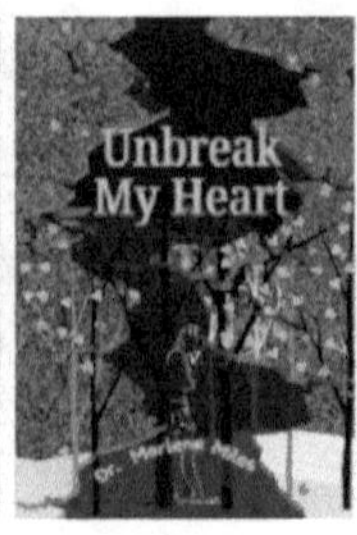

Thieves of Darkness series

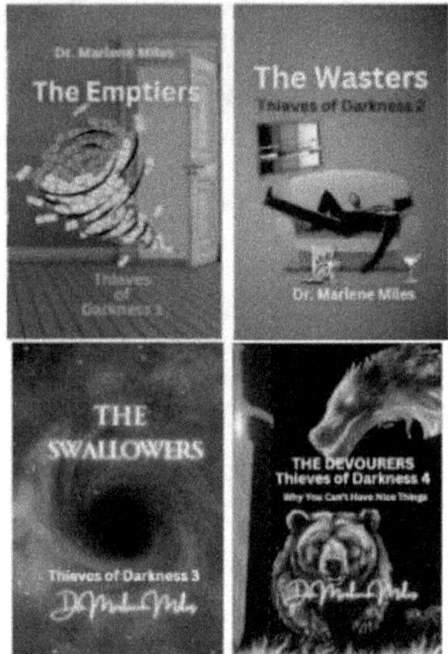

The Emptiers https://a.co/d/heio0dO

The Wasters https://a.co/d/5TG1iNQ

The Swallowers https://a.co/d/1jWhM6G

The Devourers: Why We Can't Have Nice Things
https://a.co/d/87Tejbf

Spiritual Thieves

Red Flags: The Track Is Not Safe (book & workbook)

Triangular Powers https://a.co/d/aUCjAWC

Upgrade (series) *How to Get Out of Survival Mode* https://a.co/d/aTERhXO

We Get Along, Right? Compatibility for Couples – (book & workbook)

Dr. Marlene Miles is a teacher, author, and spiritual thinker known for her grounded, discerning approach to prayer and spiritual formation. Her work emphasizes clarity, restraint, and maturity in faith—helping believers move beyond emotionalism and performance into a steady, practiced walk with God.

With a deep respect for Scripture and a practical understanding of daily life, Dr. Miles writes for those who want their prayer life to be formed, not dramatized. Her teaching encourages spiritual maintenance, discernment, and responsibility—so faith remains strong not only in crisis, but in everyday living.

www.ingramcontent.com/pod-product-compliance
Lightning Source LLC
LaVergne TN
LVHW010948110826
845149LV00015B/3256

* 9 7 8 1 9 7 1 9 3 3 4 2 9 *